Once Upon a Rhyme

Sussex

Edited by Helen Davies
& Claire Tupholme

First published in Great Britain in 2011 by:

Young Writers
Remus House
Coltsfoot Drive
Peterborough
PE2 9BF
Telephone: 01733 890066
Website: www.youngwriters.co.uk

All Rights Reserved
Book Design by Tim Christian
© Copyright Contributors 2011
SB ISBN 978-0-85739-481-1

THIS BOOK BELONGS TO

....

Foreword

Here at Young Writers our objective is to help children discover the joys of poetry and creative writing. Few things are more encouraging for the aspiring writer than seeing their own work in print. We are proud that our anthologies are able to give young authors this unique sense of confidence and pride in their abilities.

Once Upon A Rhyme is our latest fantastic competition, specifically designed to encourage the writing skills of primary school children through the medium of poetry. From the high quality of entries received, it is clear that Once Upon A Rhyme really captured the imagination of all involved.

The resulting collection is an excellent showcase for the poetic talents of the younger generation and we are sure you will be charmed and inspired by it, both now and in the future.

Contents

Maddie Stewart is our featured poet this year. She has written a nonsense workshop for you and included some of her great poems. You can find these at the end of your book.

Annecy Catholic Primary School, Seaford
Kara Hogan (8) 1
Eleanor Prout (8) 1
Kira Geoghegan (8) 2
Alice Maybury (7) 2
James Gough (8) 3
Luke Watkins (10) 3
Charlie Burns (9) 4
Sakura Smith (8) 4
Brooke Lee Wilson (7) 4
Abigail Simpson (8) 5
Jillian Kapoen (10) 5
Raúl Segura-Díaz (10) 5
Lily Silburn (9) 6

Charters Ancaster College, Bexhill-on-Sea
Matthew Ennis (10) 6
Alexandra Cheeseman (9) 7
Grace Bentley (10) 7

Christ Church CE Primary School, St Leonards-on-Sea
Eve Walker Rawson (8) 8
Tia Willson (9) 8
Joe Keep (10) 9
Isabella Pavlovich (10) 9
Felix Allsopp (9) 10
Jessica Paynter (8) 10
Amy Templeman (10) 11
Juliana Pavlovich (11) 11

Alesha Peoples (9) 12
Zdenka Stursova (9) 12
Oliver Wells (11) 13
Harrison Crane (8) 13
Louis Tomlinson (8) 13
Niamh Meston (10) 14
Gemma Griffiths (7) 14
Besiana Dauti (8) 14
Kaia Lonergan (10) 15
Olivia Gibson (8) 15
Kiara Davies (11) 15
Greta Beecroft (8) 16
Eve Adams (10) 16
Zak Willson (10) 16
Izobelle Fleckney (10) 17
Alfie Walding (10) 17
Seren Hayler (9) & John McIver 17
Chloe Bolingbroke (9) 18
Rowan Ringrose (10) 18
Josh Kinsella (10) 18
Aaron Mayatt (10) 18

Elm Grove Primary School, Brighton
Imogen Mohsin (9) 19
Joshua Buck (11) 20
Sylvie Taylor (9) 20
Tallulah Hoffmann (10) 21
Ruby Russell (10) 21
Zoë Alexander (10) 22
Andrea Defferary-Gould (7) 22
Rose Joy Preston (9) 23

Billie Nicholls (8)	23
Bella Purbrick (11)	24
Juno Phillips (9)	24
Bethany Golberg (8)	25
Roxy Sams (9)	25
Rebecca Phipps (11)	26
Alice Mary Bradley (10)	26
Mia Grassie-Clarke (10)	27
Eve Sutton (7)	27
Nina Lambert (9)	28
Emily Evans (10)	28
Zoë Parke (10)	29
Leia Belz-Koeling (9)	29
Lucas Belz-Koeling (7)	30
Bethan Roberts (9)	30
Lola Emerson (7)	30
Ruby Parker (10)	31
Kyle Greenwood (10)	31
Mira Ruiz-Cravinho (7)	32
Isabella Perrin (9)	32
Hannah Mills (8)	32
Olivia Kelly (7)	33
Eliza Sarson-Diment (11)	33
Carys Thomas (7)	33
Margaretha Cooke-Long (7)	34
Erin Freeman-Jones (11)	34
Maya Mendez (10)	34
Anya Heywood Ansell (9)	35
Daisy Tearle (8)	35
Arya Shojaian (11)	35
Ailsa Mae Hickman (10)	36
Maisie Flippance (11)	36
Abbie Hanmer (10)	36

Fittleworth Village School, Pulborough

Robert James (11)	37
Tyler Henaire (10)	37
Kacper Pawlak (11)	38
Amelia Burchell (10)	38
Guy Conners (10)	38
Talya Brash (11)	39
Holly Abell (10)	39
Harvey Aitken (11)	39

Little Common School, Bexhill-on-Sea

Tom Crathern (11)	40
Kyle Stanley (10)	40
Cassie Matthews (10)	41
Imogen Newport (11)	41
Chlöe Thompson (10)	42
Ethan Beech-Schubert	42
Tiegan Caulfield (10)	43
Cameron Praill (11)	43
Sophia Rispoli (10)	44
Molly Kemp (10)	44
Luke Soden (10)	45
Georgia Whiting (10)	45
Michael Willard (11)	46
Shania Gray (11)	46
Nicola Deans (11) & Rebecca Weston (10)	47
Eddie Rumary (10)	47
Scott Williams (10)	48
Thomas Page (10)	48
Lauren Harrod (10)	49
Zoe Wilson (11)	49
Eric Davis (10)	49

Maidenbower Junior School, Crawley

Tom Haggis (10)	50
Angel Foster (10)	51

Patcham Junior School, Brighton

Victoria Potter (7)	51
Lauren Shields (7)	52
Marcus Taylor (7)	52
Finlay Moore (8)	53
Bayley Dorrington (7)	53
Poppy Wells (8)	54
Gracie-Ella Hassani (7)	54
Rachel Smith (7)	55
Cydney Crumbie (7)	55
Daniel Jones (8)	56
Jessica Cobby (7)	56
Anna Lawson (7)	57
Freddie Eriksson (8)	57
Halle Vince (7)	58

Daisy Chilton (7) ... 58
Taylor Hale (8) ... 59
Stanley Turner (7) ... 59
Freya Downs (8) ... 60
Mia Rahilly (7) ... 60
Tom Satchwell (7) ... 61
Alex Rathbone (7) ... 61
Reece Irvine (7) ... 62
Luke Wakeford (7) ... 62
Phoebe Megan Merrington (8) ... 63
Cooper Kryskiw (7) ... 63
Dominic Lock (8) ... 64
Oakley Mountney-James (7) ... 64
Oscar Saunders (8) ... 65
Shauna Timoney (8) ... 65
Madeleine Fitzjohn-Scott (8) ... 66
Poppy Tullett (8) ... 66
Aaron Finney (8) ... 67
Sam Fowler (8) ... 67
Reuben Chilcott (7) ... 68
Jamie Nixon (7) ... 68
Jude Kensall (8) ... 69
Joseph Henty (8) ... 69
Jude Johnston (7) ... 70
Jasmine Stantiford (8) ... 70
Ewan Hook (7) ... 71
Elvie Lawden (7) ... 71
Lucy Meighan (8) ... 72
Izzy Chitty (7) ... 72
Summer Pearson (8) ... 73
Joel Hubbard (8) ... 73
Liam Bennett (8) ... 74
Lily-Joy Bywaters (8) ... 74
Lexy Bennett (7) ... 75
Harvey Bostock (7) ... 75
Ben Yates (7) ... 75
Lukas Bougas (8) ... 76
Gemma Rosam (7) ... 76
Henry Simpson (7) ... 76
Thomas Owen (7) ... 77
Hermione Barrey (7) ... 77
Faith Sampson (7) ... 77
George Sumoreeah (8) ... 78
Gracie Pratt (7) ... 78
Findley Durrant (7) ... 78
Alfie Grove (8) ... 79
Fred Hoyle (8) ... 79
Jessica Joseph (8) ... 79
Lewis Russell (7) ... 80
Abbie Bartlett (7) ... 80

Plaistow & Kirdford Primary School, Plaistow

Madeleine Brockwell (9) ... 80
Leon White (10) ... 81
Phoebe Mattison (9) ... 82
Samuel Vines (9) ... 83
Nicholas Sutton (9) ... 83
Max Ragusa (9) ... 84
Jared Allerton (10) ... 84
Kalamea Cropper (9) ... 85
Joseph Russell (9) ... 85
George Hardy (9) ... 86
Alex Jeffery (9) ... 86
Marcus Davies (9) ... 87
John Carter (10) ... 87
James Weston (10) ... 87
Elsie Wadey (10) ... 88
Connor Steer (9) ... 88
Alice Sheil (9) ... 88
Mollie-Anna Douglas (10) ... 89

Rocks Park Primary School, Uckfield

Christian Martin (11) ... 89
Gregory Lewis Ledward (9) ... 90
Louis Bissett (9) ... 90
Robert Ross (10) ... 91
Emily Morrall (7) ... 91
Zaveri Shah-Smith (10) ... 92
Nathan Dowding (8) ... 92
Joshua Yexley (8) ... 93
Ben French (10) ... 93
Katie Nettleton (10) ... 93
Katie Davies (10) ... 94
Maisie Morey (9) ... 94
Alex Marsh (8) ... 94
Callum Coe (8) ... 95
Bethany Hale (8) ... 95
Aimee Standing (7) ... 95
Joshua Stafford (9) ... 96
Tommy Jay Taylor (9) ... 96

Lorna Birkby (7)	96
Heidi Victoria Lane (8)	97
Louis Whitehead (7)	97
Chloe Florence Costar (8)	97
Thomas Nettleton (7)	98
Thomas Quinney	98
Shane Harper (8)	98
Luke Horne (9)	99
Robbie William Thomas (9)	99
Alexander Beaven (8)	99
Katie Ruben (9)	100
Michael Brimacombe (9)	100
Sam Brimacombe (7)	100
Joseph Daniel Love (8)	100
Tyler Creech (11)	101
Leo Ferguson (9)	101
Aarron Neal-Grigg	101
Saul Cannadine (7)	101
Ethan Dadswell (8)	102
Scott O'Hara (9)	102
James Shannon (8)	102
Catherine Waldock (9)	102
Sully Willis-Gil (8)	103
Emma Bernice Leycester	103
Harry Beeney (9)	103
Luca Baden (7)	103
Ashley Geary (9)	104
Ben Rowsell (10)	104
Beth Beasley (10)	104
Andrew Stears (9)	104
Torben Rose (9)	104
Jules Dieleman (9)	105
Alexandra White (10)	105
Freya Baldock	105
Benjamin Littmoden (10)	105

St Wilfrid's CE Primary School, Haywards Heath

Emily Konig (7)	105
Fay Hodson (10)	106
Emma Pendry (9)	106
Natasha Purchas & Sophie Bloomer (10)	107
Finley Rickard (10)	107
Gemma Batchelor (9)	108
Erin Ross (10)	108
Freya Goodchild (8)	109

Joe Goodchild (11)	109
Amber Tranter (9)	110
Hayden Lunn (10)	110
Adam Palmer (9)	110
Isabelle Searle (11)	111
Patrick Baxter (9)	111
Luke Bates (8)	111

Stafford Junior School, Eastbourne

Alicia Drinkwater (10)	112
Kimberly Irons (10)	113
Joshua Hackney-Ring (9)	114
Arietty Powell (10)	115
Oliver Message (10)	116
Harry O'Neil Hughes (9)	116
Kiera-Mai Capon (9)	117
Danielle Morgan (9)	117
Adam Milsom Smith (10)	118
George Cooper (10)	118
James Bown & Connor Summerfield (10)	119
Amy Clarke (9)	119
Ellie Mizen (9)	120
Aaron Clarke (10)	120
Jasmine Loats (10)	121
Samuel Eade (9)	121
Dennie Bull (10)	122
Aidan Ripley (10)	122
Jevan Luke Cousins (9)	123
Ryan Winters (9)	123
Jacob Norris (10)	124
Valentina Pescatore (9)	124
Jason Grave-Dawson (10)	125
Imam Houssein Barrientos (10)	125
Rachel Marley (9)	126
Helena Jeffery (9)	126
Grace Maynard (10)	127
Kirsty Sammes (9)	127
Emily Tucknott (10)	128
Jasmine Ward (10)	128
Sapphira Nicole Christoforou (9)	129
Ernie Pownall (10)	129
Scott Jeffery (9)	130
Luke Lawrence (10)	130
Jamie Rennie (10)	130
Mollie Macdonald (9)	131

Francesca Tann (10)	131
Oliver Thom (9)	131
Daniel James Carter (10)	132
Isabella Davy (9)	132
Rebecca Tyhurst (10)	132
Joshua Luis Da Silva (10)	133
Joshua Prysor-Jones (10)	133
Giorgia Lauren Olding (10)	133

The Globe Primary School, Lancing

Frances Romain (11)	134
Emma Downs & Rebecca Collins (8)	134
Sarah James-Short (11)	135
Henry Marchant (8)	135
Olivia Cheung (9)	136
Jay Southon (7) & Lewis James-Short (8)	136
Ethan Taylor (8)	137
Phoenix Grice & Saren Driscoll (9)	137
Terri Ballard (9)	138
Melissa Shaw (9)	138
Milly Rose Marshall (8)	139
Caitlin Wattam (8) & Lauren Redding (9)	139
Lauren Blann (8)	139
Tess Bell & Ethan Gravett (8)	140
Holly Atkinson (8)	140
Hannah Schaffa & Connor Purcell (9)	140
Jay Southon (7)	141
Caitlin Wattam (8)	141
Lucy Drake (8)	141
Billie-Jo Chandler (9)	142
Holly Atkinson & George Bartlett (8)	142
Imogen Bromley (9)	142
Terri Ballard & Jamie Peacock (9)	143
Tyla Guile (9)	143
Phoebe Jean Mayhew (9)	143

West St Leonards Primary School, St Leonards-on-Sea

Briony Thornton (10)	144
Megan-Louise Masters (11)	145
Ellie Johnson (9)	146
Beulah Griffiths Thompson (9)	147
Zoe Crowley (10)	148
Chloe Fletcher (10)	149
Imi Bennett (10)	150

Kira Jade Madge (11)	151
Rebecca Perkins (11)	151
Rian McDonald (10)	152
Nadia Avery (10)	153
Michael Amos (10)	154
Olivia Metalle (9)	155
Hannah Chapman (8)	156
Bronwyn Kent (11)	157
Megan Green (8)	158
Ryan Lucas (7)	158
Layla Constable (10)	159
Jessica Avery (8)	159
Sinead Bedwell (11)	160
Megan Barnett (11)	160
Jazmine Murray (11)	161
Natalie Stoodley (11)	161
Layla Fisher (8)	162
Sophie O'Hara (8)	162
Hamza Husain (8)	163
Kiera Dixon (10)	163
Dionne Clarke (10)	164
Hermione White (8)	164
Lydia Smith (10)	165
Joy Overbury (11)	165
Bethany McDonald (8)	166
Emily Louise Hendy (10)	166
Megan Croucher (11)	167
Joanne Perkins (9)	168

The Poems

The Two Little Squirrels

'I need some nuts,' the little squirrel said.
'To eat when it's cold and I'm tucked up in bed.'
He looked high and low, but only found one.
He hunted all around but they were gone.
'Where could they be? There should be loads.
They're not badgers, mice or toads!'
That's when he saw a little squirrel girl,
With lovely big teeth as white as pearls.
She had in her arms acorns aplenty.
There must have been ten or maybe twenty.
'Give me some nuts!' the little squirrel shouted.
She looked at him in surprise and pouted.
'Don't be so rude. I'm not in the mood.
I need these nuts for my winter's food.'
'Please, oh please!' the little squirrel cried.
'I've only got one - I really have tried!'
She smiled at him kindly, for she really was caring.
And that's how the squirrels ended up sharing.

Kara Hogan (8)
Annecy Catholic Primary School, Seaford

Firework

Fireworks sparkling,
Fireworks fizzing,
Fireworks everywhere!
Colours glistening in the air,
Rockets popping and banging,
Fizzing and whizzing,
Bang!
Bang!
Bang!
Go the sparkles in the sky.
The smoke twirling and whirling,
Spinning playfully in the air,
Children having such fun,
But they wish they had a choccy bun!

Eleanor Prout (8)
Annecy Catholic Primary School, Seaford

The Sun And The Moon

Sun
When people are awaking and the mice are sleeping,
A great merry face rose out of the sky,
He was a brilliant light,
More greater than the moon last night,
He was the son of the moon,
And rules the heavens with great power,
And blooms every morning like a flower.

Moon
When all the people are asleep,
And the little mice are beginning to creep,
A big friendly smile came out of the heavens,
She was as beautiful as a rose,
And as cheerful as a berry.
Shining light, shining bright,
She called out:
'Let all wishes come true *tonight!*'

Kira Geoghegan (8)
Annecy Catholic Primary School, Seaford

The Grumpy Owl

The animals lived in a big green wood
In the wood an old oak tree stood
And in the oak tree lived an owl.

His eyes were big and he liked to growl
The animals didn't like him one ounce
Because at night he liked to pounce.

He flies around at night over trees
And in the morning he sniffs the bees
Then one night he met a mouse coming out of his cosy house.

The mouse looked up and said to the owl,
'Why are you so terribly foul?'
The owl looked down, feeling bad
And then he said, 'I do feel sad!'

The mouse offered to be his friend
And that's what they were in the end.

Alice Maybury (7)
Annecy Catholic Primary School, Seaford

The Moon River

The moon river,
Glowing in the night,
The moon didn't stop shining,
Because it was so bright.
The moon river,
Was such a lovely sight,
Because of its light,
Still glittering in the night.
The moon river,
Shimmering so brightly,
You could not see that sight,
Because of that stillness,
It made a beautiful light.

James Gough (8)
Annecy Catholic Primary School, Seaford

Squirrel

In came a squirrel in the barber's shop,
His teeth like a dagger
Chop, chop, chop
Next to the gerbil he angrily stood,
Not being evil, not being good
It was soon his turn to sit on the chair,
Snarling madly deeply aware,
In came the hedgehog with a pointy razor,
Red eyes shining liked a two-barrelled laser,
As the razor came to his hide,
He just found out he was being spied,
A hedgehog was hiding by the door
He just found out the haircuts are poor!

Luke Watkins (10)
Annecy Catholic Primary School, Seaford

My Dog Taco

Taco is so funny
She loves to eat honey
I like to walk her in the park
I know she will protect me even in the dark
If someone comes near me when we are out
Soon they will be in trouble, because Taco's about.
I am very clean
I pick up her poo
Just like a keeper in the zoo.
I know she will always be my friend
As dogs are loyal till the end.

Charlie Burns (9)
Annecy Catholic Primary School, Seaford

Hello Kitty

H ello Kitty is
E xactly a star
L ots of people
L ike her
O nly because she is

K ittytastic
I love Hello Kitty
T hough she might not be popular in different countries
T he stars are like her
Y et she's always my hero!

Sakura Smith (8)
Annecy Catholic Primary School, Seaford

The Sky

A star, a star, I dream of the stars.
The wind, the wind, I love the wind.
The sun, the sun, the beautiful sun.
The moon, the moon, is the light of the night.
I dream, I dream, that I could fly upon the sky.
The colours of the sky light up in the sky.

Brooke Lee Wilson (7)
Annecy Catholic Primary School, Seaford

Rainbows

In the rainbow the colours are so bright,
Just like a ball of light.
A colour in the rainbow is blue,
I know because I stuck it on there with some glue.
Rainbows look very pretty,
Just like a cute kitty.
At the end of every rainbow there is a pot of gold,
I don't know if it's true but that's what I got told.
A leprechaun guards the gold,
I hope he has a tight hold.

Abigail Simpson (8)
Annecy Catholic Primary School, Seaford

A Poem About Chocolate Milk

Chocolate milk is yummy
It makes my tummy go all funny
I jump about and scream and shout on my mum's sofa.
When I spill it my mum will kill it
And send me to my room.
I will scream and shout and jump all about
If I don't get my chocolate milk soon!
My friends all love it and stuff it
As much as they can in their mouths.
They get it and drink but all I wish for is to sink (in it).

Jillian Kapoen (10)
Annecy Catholic Primary School, Seaford

Football Days

Football is a game with twenty-two people, two goals, and one ball.
It's fun, you run, you pass the ball and try to score.
Some players are tall, others small, some are fast and skilful, and others are strong and broad.
When you score a goal you can celebrate, the crowd roar, the opposition frown when they are one-nil down.
I enjoy winning, I accept losing, but the most important thing is to play the game.

Raúl Segura-Díaz (10)
Annecy Catholic Primary School, Seaford

My Cat Blarblar

She is as beautiful as a rose.
She is fluffy as a teddy.
She kisses me for her dinner and her breakfast too.
She snuggles me in my bed and sends me off to school.
That is my foxy lady Blarblar and we all love her too.

Lily Silburn (9)
Annecy Catholic Primary School, Seaford

Winter

Birds cough in the cold stone barn
Bonfires blaze and crackle
While cobwebs shiver
And shadows die as they fade away.

Cars sparkle in the frosty garage
Chimneys smoke in the black winter's sky
While clocks go back in the old house
And fog hangs thickly among the trees.

Rain falls as blue as the sky
Flying through the cloudy sky
Dropping to the ground
As smooth as crystal.

Falling, falling to the ground
As shiny as gold
I can hear it smashing
Like leaves crumbling.

Splash, splash, splash.

Matthew Ennis (10)
Charters Ancaster College, Bexhill-on-Sea

The Rain

The cloudburst crashed
Like shiny tins smashing
Then the rain starts to fall
Sounding like a switch
Turning quickly on and off.

Rain, fine as dust, floats in the air
A light see-through blue
Shining in the sky
Tasting like ice-cold water
Slipping down my throat

A diamond shimmering
Shining in the darkness
Falling to the wet grass
Until at last all is still and calm
Everything is quiet.

Alexandra Cheeseman (9)
Charters Ancaster College, Bexhill-on-Sea

Rain

Raindrops sound like beads
Dropping onto a glass table
Upside-down helium-free balloons
Tasting like a dissolving sweet in my mouth.
A see-through tear like a shining star
Feeling like a slithering snake
In my cold hands
Making a deep lagoon
Where frogs and fish swim.

Grace Bentley (10)
Charters Ancaster College, Bexhill-on-Sea

Snow

Snow, snow, the wonder of the world,
Throw snowballs. Go!
And throw
Show that you are the best.
Snow is freezing,
So you might notice when you are sneezing!

Finding freezing icicles
Don't stop to show.

Snowflakes are like
Stars glittery, shiny stars.
Snow, snowflakes are like
Glittering fairies,
Icicles cold as Antarctica.

Frost, frost, crunchy as caves,
Caves, caves.
Beautiful and mysterious
And delirious too.

Snow, snow twirling and whirling
Like a tornado.
Magical snowflakes like
Shining diamonds.
Snow, snow, white as the moon.

Eve Walker Rawson (8)
Christ Church CE Primary School, St Leonards-on-Sea

Compassion

C aring for . . .
O thers less fortunate.
M aking a difference to their lives.
P utting their needs before yours,
A nd saving them from poverty.
S howing that you care.
S o that they know you are there.
I know we can make a difference.
O nly a few pence each to end
N onsense and a life of struggle.

Tia Willson (9)
Christ Church CE Primary School, St Leonards-on-Sea

Trees Are . . .

Trees are tall
In their branches birds call
But then one day a tree will fall
Then no birds in their branches call at all.

Trees are green
On their branches nuts are seen
Then soon after the nuts have been
And on trees you can be keen.

Trees are strong
Their lives are long
They do nothing wrong
If they could sing they'd sing a mournful song.

Trees are also brown
If they could they would frown
It's awful when they get cut down
And in a flood they will drown.

Trees are cool
They suck water from a pool
People cut them with a tool
People who cut them are fools.

Joe Keep (10)
Christ Church CE Primary School, St Leonards-on-Sea

If A Tree Can

If a tree can scream what would it scream for . . .
If a tree could walk where would it go . . .
If a tree could speak what would it tell us . . .
But a tree stands calm and quiet . . .
If a tree had friends who would it play with . . .
If a tree had thoughts what would it think of . . .
If a tree had a lover who would he love . . .
Still a tree stands calm and quiet . . .
If we chop them down what are we left with . . .
If we waste oxygen around us how can we live . . .
If we waste God's creation aren't we doomed . . .

So please protect our planet . . .

Isabella Pavlovich (10)
Christ Church CE Primary School, St Leonards-on-Sea

A Willow Tree

A willow tree has heard many things
Lots of secrets it can tell
About times of sadness and joy.

Providing shelter for the homeless
Protecting people from the rain
While the willow takes the damage.

It cries all night and all day
That is why a willow tree is called a weeping tree
And no one even notices.

The willow tree gets cut down
It probably screams an agonising scream
Yet people do not care.

Tall and strong
Calm and gentle
Sorrow and joy
A few words to describe a willow tree.

Felix Allsopp (9)
Christ Church CE Primary School, St Leonards-on-Sea

The Snow

The snow, the snow is falling down,
I like snow, it's silent, it's fun,
I go sledging in Alexandra Park, that's one.
Brrrr. I wear my winter clothes
Hat, scarf, gloves, coat, now off we go!
I see icicles, hear them banging
On the ground, *bang, bang,* they're falling down.
I'm slip-sliding everywhere.
It gives me colds, *aaaachooooo!*
I nearly froze my nose!
I see sparkles glazing at me
Shimmering upon the ice.
I see beautiful sights looking at me
Upon winter's lights.

Jessica Paynter (8)
Christ Church CE Primary School, St Leonards-on-Sea

The Oak Tree

The oak tree is the best place to me.
From its long wavy branches to its delicate leaves.
The oak tree is the best place to me.

The oak tree is the best place to me.
The quietness of its breathing which stops when cut down.
The oak tree is the best place to me.

The oak tree is the best place to me.
It whispers to its friends and waves to say bye.
The oak tree is the best place to me.

The oak tree is the best place to me.
The way it stays calm, the way it stays alive.
The oak tree is the best place to me.

Amy Templeman (10)
Christ Church CE Primary School, St Leonards-on-Sea

Remember The Pier

As I see the pier burn down,
My heart burns down with it.
It used to dip its toes into the sea
And I did too.

I remember its groovy moves
And its relaxing sounds.
I remember its stomach;
I used to dance in there.

I loved the pier,
It was a part of me.
I know deep down, in its heart;
That it loves me.

Juliana Pavlovich (11)
Christ Church CE Primary School, St Leonards-on-Sea

Secret Tree Holder

I go to a tree to tell all my secrets
And it never replies back to me.

Whenever I tell my secret to the tree
It shakes, it leans left to right.

I go to a tree every day to tell new secrets to it
And it never replies back.

At night-time I get lonely and scared
Bu,t oh well, the tree is still next to me when I'm in bed.

I still say secrets to it when I'm in bed
I'm going to have it next to me all the time
Even when I'm in bed.

Alesha Peoples (9)
Christ Church CE Primary School, St Leonards-on-Sea

Sway Front And Back

I sway front and back all the time.
The only thing I hear is tears of goodbye.
I never thought I'd be a tree with branches so wide.
If I was a person I'd be good at things like counting leaves
And making friends play with me.
I'd be good at maths especially counting trees.
I look in the window and see a TV with people cutting down trees.
If I was a kid my mum would hold my hand.
If I was a kid I'd play tag.
My wish is not to fall down on the ground
Or I'll say bye-bye.

Zdenka Stursova (9)
Christ Church CE Primary School, St Leonards-on-Sea

The Old Man

He is a rock, battered by tyrant ocean.

Each year a fragment of his tattered body falls
And creates a new grain of sand.

He is laden by the weight of his old age:
It is a burden too hard to bear.

The colours from his eyes darken as each day passes.

He asks why must time go so fast?
Because it is ferociously gnawing at his heart,
Making him old.

Oliver Wells (11)
Christ Church CE Primary School, St Leonards-on-Sea

Let It Snow

Snow as white as a cauliflower,
Smooth as a piece of paper,
White as whipped cream,
Cold as a freezer,
Powdery as a flour,
Cold as the coldest ice,
Snow as white as the moon,
Chalets covered in snow,
Like tiny Toblerone bars
Floating in milkshake.

Harrison Crane (8)
Christ Church CE Primary School, St Leonards-on-Sea

Snowflakes

Snowflakes drift ever so fast
They sparkle and sparkle,
When will it snow, oh when?

At last it starts to snow
The snow is ever so fast
But there's one thing that I don't like about the snow
It is so freezing!

Louis Tomlinson (8)
Christ Church CE Primary School, St Leonards-on-Sea

The Pumpkin

We carved the pumpkin
Two eyes, a nose and a mouth
He began to smile.
We put a candle in his mouth
He smiled more, and his eyes lit up.
In the dark, the flickering flame began to dance.
On the walls, shadows leaped and jumped around.
With the heat, his face took on a ghoulish smile.
The cat walked past, the eyes followed.
We blew the candle out, he lost his smile.

Niamh Meston (10)
Christ Church CE Primary School, St Leonards-on-Sea

Snow

Silent snow you'll love to go
As silent as you'll ever know
We can't go on our bicycles
Because there's loads of icicles
The snow is very deep
It makes the children all asleep
Icy cold, icy cold, snow so light
Icy cold, icy cold, it is so white
The snow is as white as vanilla ice cream (yum!)
It's really not a dream.

Gemma Griffiths (7)
Christ Church CE Primary School, St Leonards-on-Sea

Snow

Cocoons nestled like chocolate,
Crunchy biscuits in whipped cream.
Fur trees as snowy as white candyfloss,
Chalets covered in white sparkly sugar.
The snow is as white as icing sugar.
It is as cosy as a quilt.
The snow is as cold as a freezer.

Besiana Dauti (8)
Christ Church CE Primary School, St Leonards-on-Sea

The Poem Of A Juniper Tree

I once stood there on a ranch.
While birds were pecking on my branch.
While everyone was having a dance.
I looked to my left then right, I did myself have a chance.
And them squirrels gave me a dare, I don't care.
I think I would shrink at that strange commotion.
The low sounds in the distance creep me.
I stand tall not realising the fall.
Now my trunk and branches are gone.
For I am now a lowly stall.

Kaia Lonergan (10)
Christ Church CE Primary School, St Leonards-on-Sea

Compassion Acrostic Poem

C aring for other people
O ffering a chance to share feelings
M aking a good friend
P ray for the less fortunate
A compassionate person has a kind and caring heart
S how love and mercy
S hare with the poor
I f someone is upset go and show friendship
O pen to people's feelings
N o one stops giving compassion.

Olivia Gibson (8)
Christ Church CE Primary School, St Leonards-on-Sea

Remember The Pier

Remember the pier,
The old dancing club,
The yummy sweet shop,
But now he's all alone,
Furious and tired,
Surviving on his old knees.
Remember the pier.

Kiara Davies (11)
Christ Church CE Primary School, St Leonards-on-Sea

In The Snow

Snow as white as icing sugar.
Icing sugar as tasty as a candy cane.
Snow covers the chalets.
Snow that looks like white marshmallow.
Snow as white as mashed potatoes.
Ice just like slippery sleet.
Chalets like they're in a milkshake bed.
Tree shadows look like icicles.
Fluffy snow like the fur of a white rabbit.

Greta Beecroft (8)
Christ Church CE Primary School, St Leonards-on-Sea

What A Lovely Tree

What a lovely tall tree
Hopefully it won't fall on me, it grows lemons
And when you eat them
It feels like you're in heaven
I wonder how deep the root goes
And just look at that frog leap around it
I wish trees were free like me and if it was free it would be able to run a marathon with me
What a beautiful tree which is suitable for me.

Eve Adams (10)
Christ Church CE Primary School, St Leonards-on-Sea

The Lighthouse

Lonely, he stands.
This tall, shadowy figure.
Watching,
Waiting,
Anticipating.
The unpredictable, that is the sea.
Weathered and beaten by the waves.
Expecting nothing in return from those he saves.
The lighthouse.

Zak Willson (10)
Christ Church CE Primary School, St Leonards-on-Sea

Suspicion

Her head makes up the universe
    And she hides it all away.
Her eyes make up the moon
    Which glows and shines at night.
When the night-time comes her little starry
    Fingers go up to the sky.
Only she knows the truth,
    If there is life on other planets,
Worlds unrecognised.

Izobelle Fleckney (10)
Christ Church CE Primary School, St Leonards-on-Sea

Perfect Trees All Around Me

They are everywhere
But what I don't get
Is that some people cut down this magnificence
But you can't let them
And soon we will forget
So we must stop this insanity
Before we will regret.

Alfie Walding (10)
Christ Church CE Primary School, St Leonards-on-Sea

Sam The Tree

My leaves are small
But my trunk is very tall.
My little branches fall but I'm still cool.
Day or night I always have perfect sight.
I am very strong and my branches are very long.
That is just me.
I am Sam the tree.

Seren Hayler (9) & John McIver
Christ Church CE Primary School, St Leonards-on-Sea

One Leaf

A tree is a wonderful place to be
Whenever you get lonely.

I play there every day and I say
This is the best place to be!

The tree is important to me
It is like family that's why I love the tree!

Chloe Bolingbroke (9)
Christ Church CE Primary School, St Leonards-on-Sea

A Tree Wandering Free

A tree, a simple but gentle being wandering free,
A spruce, pine, a juniper or lime.
It's always there for me. They have witnessed everything,
Know all the secrets of the world. A tree, a friend for life
Just wandering free. Old but strong, tall but kind.
It's always there for me.

Rowan Ringrose (10)
Christ Church CE Primary School, St Leonards-on-Sea

The Tree

The tree gazing at the bright red sun,
On the hill drenched with green flowered grass,
As his leaves float in the gushing wind,
Letting his root fall into the ground
And while the tree stands its ground.

Josh Kinsella (10)
Christ Church CE Primary School, St Leonards-on-Sea

The Old Tree

In the holidays the tree was old
I saw the tree with my family
When we were going shopping
I was really excited about going back to school
It is school, woo-hoo it's gardening.

Aaron Mayatt (10)
Christ Church CE Primary School, St Leonards-on-Sea

Tormenting Toucan's Trouble

Tormenting toucan was bored one day sitting in his tree,
So he started trilling at the animals that he could see.
'The jaguar, the jaguar he's journeying this way,
The jaguar, the jaguar he'll eat you up today.'
Twelve pairs of beady eyes looked up in alarm,
Most began to scurry and only one was calm.
The sleepy sloth he couldn't run for he was far too slow,
So he slumbered snoozily on his way as fast as he could go.

Tormenting toucan sat and laughed for it was all a joke,
He felt his power growing so then again he spoke.
'The jaguar, the jaguar, he's journeying this way,
The jaguar, the jaguar he'll eat you up today.'
A tiny timid tree frog looked with terrified round eyes,
He tiptoed trembling across the branch to put on his disguise.

Slithering sly snake patted toucan soundlessly on the head,
'Do it again, it's funny, they think they'll all be dead!'
'The jaguar, the jaguar, he's journeying this way,
The jaguar, the jaguar, he'll eat you up today.'
The light-footed lizard leapt and hid inside a crack,
He wouldn't let that jaguar have him for his morning snack.

Tormenting toucan laughed with glee and slithering sly snake giggled,
'Again, again!' Snake shouted out while the tree began to jiggle.
'The jaguar, the jaguar, he's journeying this way,
The jaguar, the jaguar, he'll eat you up today.'
'Attention!' shouted an army of ants as they hid they chorused, 'Hooray.'
Whilst truthful trotting tapir was triumphant at his get away.

Tormenting toucan and sly snake continued with their game,
But what they didn't see was really such a shame.
The other animals stopped and stared but toucan couldn't see,
That behind him the journeying jaguar was sitting on the tree!

Imogen Mohsin (9)
Elm Grove Primary School, Brighton

Swoosh, Swoosh Went The Sea

Swoosh, swoosh,
Went the sea,
He was woken by a shipwreck.
He remembered he was angry last night,
But he really did not know why.
Swoosh, swoosh,
Went the sea,
He groaned as he got up.
He could not get up,
The crabs were dragging him down.
Swoosh, swoosh,
Went the sea,
He saw a dam.
He swelled up with anger,
He smashed the dam down.
Swoosh, swoosh,
Went the sea,
He was desperate to play.
He hurled a fish at the Pacific. No response.
He was bored, more bored than ever,
Swoosh, swoosh,
Went the sea.
Swoosh, swoosh,
Swoosh, swoosh,
Went . . .
The . . .
Sea . . .

Joshua Buck (11)
Elm Grove Primary School, Brighton

Jellied Pupils

Spill the beans on Robin and Dean.
Make jelly of Lauren and Ellie.
Stir Sid and Hugh up in a stew.
Put custard with Florry and Nelly.
Roast Lilly in the oven with gravy made of Davey.
Why not add fruit salad to the mix? Secret ingredient - a bit of Nick.
Oh poor little Miss Loop is stuck right inside the soup.

Sylvie Taylor (9)
Elm Grove Primary School, Brighton

The Night Of Fright

The silver moon looks down
On the deep dark woods
On this night of fright and scares
So if you stride out for a stroll
In these deep dark woods
Then look out! Watch out! Beware!

For all is not right
On this mysterious night;
Evil is out on the prowl
The spirits are about
The wind howls like a banshee
And the smell of death is strong and foul.

So don't be fooled
By the swirling fog
As it dances you wrong-ways
You will be lost in the forest of terror
Frozen in a petrified daze
So watch out! Watch out!
You won't want to be seen!
On this night of evil!
It's . . .
Halloween!

Tallulah Hoffmann (10)
Elm Grove Primary School, Brighton

A Beautiful Thing

Each summer I see butterflies
As silent as the dark blue night,
Gliding through the soft, warm, translucent air.
Then I have this magical moment,
One brave butterfly gently lands
On my finger's edge.
I gaze in wonder at the design of the bewitching wings.
I hold my breath and marvel at this miracle.
But the next time I look down to see
This enchanting creature, all that remains
Is a beautiful memory.

Ruby Russell (10)
Elm Grove Primary School, Brighton

A Guinea Pig

I went to the shop to get
A furry, fluffy guinea pig pet
Which should I choose?
One that sings the blues?
A scary guinea pig, a hairy guinea pig
Or a fairy guinea pig?
A sad guinea pig, a bad guinea pig
Or a mad guinea pig?
A king guinea pig, a ring guinea pig
Or a sing a sing sing guinea pig?
A smelly guinea pig, a telly guinea pig
Or a big, big belly guinea pig?
A grumpy guinea pig, a lumpy guinea pig
Or a jumpy guinea pig?
A brown guinea pig, a blue guinea pig
An old guinea pig or a new guinea pig?
I chose one that was happy and wore a nappy
Another who was snappy
And three more that were cheeky, leaky and sleepy.

Zoë Alexander (10)
Elm Grove Primary School, Brighton

How The Cat Got The Hat

A man walked along in a hat
He was tired so on a bench he sat
He then fell asleep, off dropped his hat
When along came a scruffy-looking rat.

The rat saw the hat and said, 'I'm having that'
So put it on his head with a happy little pat
Then along came a hungry looking cat
With a smile he saw a rat in a hat.

The cat chased after the rat
The rat ran away dropping the hat
The rat was too fast for the cat
So the cat had to make do with the hat.

And that is how the cat got the hat
How about that!

Andrea Defferary-Gould (7)
Elm Grove Primary School, Brighton

My Dream Car

Let me tell you about my dream car,
It'll take me places near and far,
It will be a Cadillac,
The colour of it will be black.

It will have an open top roof,
And it will be waterproof,
People will come from far and wide,
To see me and my car by my side.

Many, many years go by,
As they pass they seem to fly,
I suppose I'll never get my car,
To take me places near and far.

This dream never will come true,
I've had lots of good ones and
Some bad ones too,
Many dreams I've had were real,
So I think I've had a very good deal.

Rose Joy Preston (9)
Elm Grove Primary School, Brighton

Grin And Bear It

Bad things happen a lot at school
Like when Alicen put worms in the swimming pool
They wriggled in my swimsuit and around my legs
I got out of the pool and worms fell to the floor
I hoped Brandon and his gang didn't see
But they did and I've been bullied since
Bashed and bruised and punched and kicked
The way forward is to grin and bear it
But then one day I'd had enough
I told the head teacher Mr Gruff
The strictest teacher in the school
Mean, angry and really cruel
He told them off real bad
And then they told Brandon's dad
And all is happy now,
I hope.

Billie Nicholls (8)
Elm Grove Primary School, Brighton

A Fright In The Night

There's a monster under my bed
I wish it was a bunny instead.

It moans and groans in the night
And it always gives me a fright.

The howling and growling is so scary
It's probably really hairy.

I slowly lower my head
Underneath the bed.

It's never-ending black
I take a step back.

It comes closer
And closer
And closer
Until . . .
Woof!
And a tiny puppy creeps out.

Bella Purbrick (11)
Elm Grove Primary School, Brighton

You're Out Of My Life

I can't sleep.
I can't eat.
Because you're out of my life.
You pushed me aside and walked off into the street and left me on the pavement.
If you came back.
I'd love you to bits and I'd never leave your side
Because I love you, yes I do. I love you.
When I met you
I thought, *is this real?* My lip started to shake
First you asked me out, I said yes.
But after you left me.
I did not know what to do
I cried and cried for days.
Until I saw you with her.
I knew you were out of my life.

Juno Phillips (9)
Elm Grove Primary School, Brighton

My Cousin Leo

My cousin Leo is really sweet
The cutest baby you will ever meet
He loves to kiss and to cuddle
He sometimes gets into a muddle.

My cousin Leo is lots of fun
He learned to walk but he wanted to run
He loves to jump on the bed
He doesn't care if he bangs his head.

My cousin Leo loves to play
He pushes his buggy around all day
But there is something he likes more
Things with buttons, remote controls, cor!

My cousin Leo pulls my hair
It hurts a bit but he doesn't care
He is stubborn, his first word was 'no'
But I love him even so.

Bethany Golberg (8)
Elm Grove Primary School, Brighton

Shooting Star

When I see a shooting star
I wish for a shiny car.

I wish for something cool
Like a swimming pool.

I wish for clothes, shoes and toys
And things that make lots of noise.

I know I should wish for love and peace
But sometimes I just feel like a quiche.

So come on, shooting star
Whether you are near or far.

I hope to see you very soon
Maybe even from my room.

I want to make a wish
Even if it's just for a special dish.

Roxy Sams (9)
Elm Grove Primary School, Brighton

Oh, What To Write?

I was sitting in class one rainy day,
When my teacher began to say,
My ears pricked up and my face lit up,
As my teacher announced a competition today.

'You can write about anything you like.
Cats or mats, flowers or powers.
Bugs or beetles, dogs or frogs.'

There is so much to choose, oh what should I do?
I sat at home and thought a while,
But my brain was feeling weary,
So I put it to bed to rest a while.

I woke in the morning and my brain went *click,*
I had an idea of what to write
I could write about thinking about a poem . . .
So I decided to write about . . .
　　This!

Rebecca Phipps (11)
Elm Grove Primary School, Brighton

Blitz!

Looking around I knew I was in Hell.
Splinters of glass flew like scorpions' tails,
Thousands of distressed people sprinting from the sea of bombs.
Fire creeping around me, blazing like burning eyeballs,
Seeping, suffocating smoke.
Air raid sirens screeching like newborn babies,
Shattering wood flying.
Rough metal of dented shelters hidden under the rubble of forgotten homes.
Fire gripping my hands,
Screaming at me.
Glimpses of the burning sun, morning, daybreak.
Coughing children emerging from lost houses,
Dead souls drifting up to Heaven.
Death, blitz!

Alice Mary Bradley (10)
Elm Grove Primary School, Brighton

Time

Time to wake up, breakfast time
No time to waste, don't hang about . . .
Squeeze out the toothpaste, two minutes brushing teeth
Out the door and up the street
Running late, church bell chimes
School bell rings at 9
Get in line
Just in time
Can't wait till break time 5 minutes left till times table test.
Teacher says we're wasting her time.
After lunch it's golden time
Have to wait, Mum's late (again)
She always seems to take her time
Half an hour computer time, into bed at quarter to 9
But don't forget story time.

Mia Grassie-Clarke (10)
Elm Grove Primary School, Brighton

My Little Pixie Friends

Dancing round the toadstools,
When the sun's not in the sky.

Skipping, playing, running around,
When the day is nearly nigh.

Climbing all the trees and playing in the breeze.
When I'm with my pixie friends the fun never ever ends.

But now the day has nearly come
It's time to end this lovely fun.

And now the night has come again,
It's time to laugh and sing and play.

Because we are the very best of friends,
And our friendship never ends.

Eve Sutton (7)
Elm Grove Primary School, Brighton

Blitz

Bombs dropping,
Blowing roofs off.
Glad I'm safe
In a deep dark shelter.
Smashing glass,
Sky armada.
Hot fire
Burns my skin.
People screaming
Bursts my eardrums.
Will I live or
Will I die or
Will I scream
And start to cry?

Nina Lambert (9)
Elm Grove Primary School, Brighton

Little Brother

Thin and slim,
Snotty and grotty,
Easily annoyed with a tap on his back.
Lack of maturity,
An old sofa sack,
Now what d'ya think about that?
Head as big as a lemon,
Or a melon too,
Old Nike trainers,
He drives us insane,
Silly cheeky smile,
Dinosaur room too,
Oh, and his artificial goo!

Emily Evans (10)
Elm Grove Primary School, Brighton

Rhymes

Once upon a time,
I thought I found a rhyme!
But it slipped away,
To be chased another day.

I looked under the sofa,
It was not there!
I looked in the cupboard
But it was bare.

I looked in the bedroom,
Hoping to find it there!
But with my luck,
I could not find it anywhere!

Zoë Parke (10)
Elm Grove Primary School, Brighton

Waterfall

Water tumbling like blue wavy hair
Into a pool at my feet.
Jagged rocks here and there
Stopping the current at its best.
Here I'm alone in a clearing of blue
With the water whispering to me,
Telling me secrets, otherwise mysteries.
It's getting dark
I have to go home
It's difficult to part with this place.
I look down at my feet
I have a tail.

Leia Belz-Koeling (9)
Elm Grove Primary School, Brighton

Chinese New Year

Chinese dragons flying through the air
Match the beautiful colours of the fair.
The red thin bodies of these mythical beasts
Represent power and good luck in the Far East.
Colours of the rainbow flying up great heights
Will be visible both day and night.
Delicious smells wafting around
Of sweet inviting jai, golden and browned.
Evil spirits go away
After the dragon dancers have their say.
Fireworks explode into the moonless night
Carrying the wish for the future to be shiny bright.

Lucas Belz-Koeling (7)
Elm Grove Primary School, Brighton

The River's Song

It is lush, it is green on the banks of the river,
Where the water rushes grow,
Where the little, tiny toad sings out his song for everyone to know.
A kingfisher dives into depths of the stream,
As his beautiful feathers begin to gleam.
Some fish leap high in the mist-filled air,
As their sparkling fins begin to glare,
The sun goes down behind the trees,
As I walk along the riverbank,
Through a gentle breeze.
And that is what I hear as I walk along
And what I hear is the river's song.

Bethan Roberts (9)
Elm Grove Primary School, Brighton

Doughnut, Doughnut, Doughnut!

Doughnut, doughnut, doughnut with icing like snow.
And yummy rainbow-coated sprinkles shining in the flow.
How I long to eat you and feel you in my belly
Yummy, yummy, yummy, scrummy, scrummy, scrummy.

Lola Emerson (7)
Elm Grove Primary School, Brighton

My Cat

Scimper, scamper my cat goes,
    Always watching on his toes,
He hunts and plays all day long,
    But when it's night he purrs me a song,
He'll chase a shadow up a wall,
    Just to get a hug is all,
His fur presses against my skin,
    In a hot-water bottle contest he'd win,
He's always there when I am sad,
    Even when I've been bad,
I give him a hug every day,
    Maybe that's why he's here to stay.

Ruby Parker (10)
Elm Grove Primary School, Brighton

The Silent Night

As the night is dark
The stars are bright
The moon shines on throughout the night
The planets are colourful, mighty and light
O my lovely pitch-black night
The comets, they soar right through my sight
As I watch the silent night
O what mysteries lie up there
Beneath the heavens and in the air?
Few people know
Few people care
For the mysteries that lie up there.

Kyle Greenwood (10)
Elm Grove Primary School, Brighton

A Tweet In A Tree

Once there was a bird
That wanted to be heard
He sat in a tree
And whistled to me
The sound was so amazing
I just stood there gazing
Then he flew to a place he knew
A worm caught his eye
He flew through the sky back to the place he knew
He went to the worm who squiggled, wriggled and turned
He thought maybe his baby would like to eat it.

Mira Ruiz-Cravinho (7)
Elm Grove Primary School, Brighton

The Fair!

It was the fair,
The police were there
She ran her fingers through her hair
She made her way
Through the tent of modelling clay
And found her way out
And without a doubt
Made her way home
Pressed the head of the garden gnome
That unlocked the door
You see she had broken the law!

Isabella Perrin (9)
Elm Grove Primary School, Brighton

Snail, Snail, Snail!

Snail, snail, snail eating all the grass
I wonder what he'll do when he finds a bit of brass.
He stares into its shiny surface
And discovers it's a mirror.
He looks and sees two googly eyes
Which sends him all aquiver!

Hannah Mills (8)
Elm Grove Primary School, Brighton

Autumn

Halloween is coming soon,
Coming out early is the moon,
The wind is making shapes and sounds,
Picking up leaves,
And dropping them down.
The days are getting shorter,
The nights are getting darker.
Spiky, green conker shells covering the ground,
Open one up and you will find a conker,
Chocolate-brown.

Olivia Kelly (11)
Elm Grove Primary School, Brighton

The Door

There's a black door in my house, which only I can see,
It creaks at night and at day,
I wonder what it could be.
Sometimes I hear scratching, scraping on the floor,
No one else believes me, about that black door.
It drifts through my mind at day, and haunts me at night,
I quiver and think constantly
What's behind that black door? Is it a terrible sight?
One day I decide, I'll go through the door.
I open it slowly; can you guess what I saw?

Eliza Sarson-Diment (11)
Elm Grove Primary School, Brighton

Mice Like Cheese

Yummy, yummy cheese
Oh please, oh please, oh please!
I'm not so fond of peas
Nor spicy hot chillies.

I'd love a cheesy slice
That is fantastically nice
A piece of chilli will make me silly
What a super silly Billy!

Carys Thomas (7)
Elm Grove Primary School, Brighton

The Flowery Love Poem

Roses are red, violets are blue,
Every time I see you
I think I fall in love with you.
Dandelions are yellow,
Daisies are white.
Every time I see you
You glitter in the sunlight.
Marigolds are orange, foxgloves are pink.
When I see you
I wish I could think.

Margaretha Cooke-Long (7)
Elm Grove Primary School, Brighton

Something To Dream Of Before I Go To Sleep

A glass banana
Some peach music
A tiny rose
A milk symphony
Some delirious power
A chocolate eternity
A honey vision
Some soul stars
A smiling planet
All is well.

Erin Freeman-Jones (11)
Elm Grove Primary School, Brighton

In The Playground

People in the playground,
Screaming really loud.
People in the playground,
Making quite a sound.
People in the playground,
Laughing, having fun.
People in the playground,
Eating currant buns.

Maya Mendez (10)
Elm Grove Primary School, Brighton

It Wasn't Me!

Splash! went the paint
'Mum, don't faint
It wasn't me, I'm only three.'

Crash! went the glass
Dad gave a gasp
'I do care but I was over there.'

Bang! went the pan
'I'm sorry Nan'
'Don't worry James we'll play some games.'

Anya Heywood Ansell (9)
Elm Grove Primary School, Brighton

Beep, Beep, Beep!

Beep, beep, beep goes the drill,
Is it ill?

Beep, beep, beep goes the till,
Is it ill?

Beep, beep, beep goes the rat,
Has it seen a cat?

Beep, beep, beep goes the cat,
Has it eaten a rat?

Daisy Tearle (8)
Elm Grove Primary School, Brighton

Silver Moon

The old man sat in his house
Looking towards the colourful grouse
Under the moon he played a tune
About his dad's doom
His plane had gone high in the sky
And had come down in a terrible boom
At first he was glad, then he was sad
Soon he went mad with grief and rage.

Arya Shojaian (11)
Elm Grove Primary School, Brighton

My Hamster Is Nutty!

My hamster ate a nut last night; he swallowed it whole, what a terrible sight.
I woke this morning to find him dead; his body ran away from his head.
I decided to give him a proper goodbye,
I prepared him a funeral and began to cry.
I wept and I wailed, I screamed and I stamped.
Why did you? How could you? Go die like that?
I never forgave him what he did that day.
He left, he went, he passed away.

Ailsa Mae Hickman (10)
Elm Grove Primary School, Brighton

Windy Wind

Wisely wind blowing side to side,
Blowing people with their pride,
Blowing people far away,
Away from where they want to be today,
Twirling round every day and running a running race,
Going here, going there, going everywhere,
Up, down, side to side, everywhere in the air.

Maisie Flippance (11)
Elm Grove Primary School, Brighton

Mr Know It All

Mr Know It All is back in town
He's tall, he's funny and has a strange sense of humour.
He's as clever as a feather that flies around me.
Mr Know It All loves to play, even on rainy days.
He loves you, he loves meeee.
We all play together nicely.
I love him and so do you.

Abbie Hanmer (10)
Elm Grove Primary School, Brighton

Doctor

The doctor calls my name.
My body starts to shiver.
My tummy swirling and spinning.

I hate injections!

He lays me down on the hospital bed.
The doctor looks in my eyes.
He can see I'm nervous.

I hate injections!

Squirt, squirt, he walks closer,
With an evil glint in his eyes.

I hate injections!

'Oucchh!' I scream. I feel queasy.
'Argh!' That wasn't bad.

I like injections!

Robert James (11)
Fittleworth Village School, Pulborough

Playing Football

Running with the ball.

Goal!

I need a drink. I'm boiling!

Goal!

Ahhh! We're never going to win!

Goal!

We're going to win, easy!

Goal!

That was brilliant son.
Clap, clap, clap.

Tyler Henaire (10)
Fittleworth Village School, Pulborough

Rugby Match

People cheering.
People kicking the ball.

'Come on! Come on!'

'What's the score?'
People tackling.

'Come on! Come on!'

Players shouting, 'Pass!'
Referee blowing his whistle.

'Come on! Come on!'

Kacper Pawlak (11)
Fittleworth Village School, Pulborough

The Train Station

I can see lots of people catching the train.
'Brrrr, it's freezing out here!'

I can hear the train coming round the bend.
'Brrr, it's freezing out here!'

I think I've missed the train.
'Brrrr, it's freezing out here!'

People chatting in the café.
'Brrrr, it's freezing out here!'

Amelia Burchell (10)
Fittleworth Village School, Pulborough

The Airport

People chatting
I can't wait for the holiday.
Aeroplane announcements
I can't wait for the holiday.
People running with suitcases
I can't wait for the holiday.
I wonder how long the journey will take?

Guy Conners (10)
Fittleworth Village School, Pulborough

Scuba-Diving

Pop! Pop! Pop!
Colourful coral all around me.
Pop! Pop! Pop!
Fish swimming past in a school.
Pop! Pop! Pop!
This is fun.
Pop! Pop! Pop!
'Oh no! I'm out of air!'
Pop!

Talya Brash (11)
Fittleworth Village School, Pulborough

The Busy Corridor

'Hey do you want to come to my house?'
'Can I sit next to you?'
Why is it so busy? *Argh!*
'Ha ha! You fell over! Ha ha!'
Teachers with angry frowns.
Why is it so busy? *Argh!*

Holly Abell (10)
Fittleworth Village School, Pulborough

Electronics

Wires, wires all around me.
Wires scraping against each other.
How am I going to fix this?
Hissing sparks flying everywhere.

Harvey Aitken (11)
Fittleworth Village School, Pulborough

If
(Inspired by 'If' by Rudyard Kipling)

If you can stay strong when others
Have no faith in you
If you can do wrong but only against your
Opponent
If you can stay optimistic but be
Realistic
When being hated
Don't give up.

If you can be proud about fighting
For your country
If you can encourage others but still
Motivate yourself
If you can be fearless but be a good man
Or being blamed
Don't give up.

If you make dreams your master
Be prepared to meet with disaster
If you can bear to hear the lies you've spoken
Be prepared to meet the broken
If you can forget what's happened before
You will rise from the floors.

Tom Crathern (11)
Little Common School, Bexhill-on-Sea

The Big, Bloody Blitz

On the dark, dull, damp night
People devastated.
Children crying while slowly
Shaking through the street.
The smoke floated lifelessly through the air like a ghost
Mums cried tears like a waterfall.
The bricks danced as the bomb hit the floor.
The buildings; towering giants,
Trembling, making shadows on the street.
It was as dark as a cave.

Kyle Stanley (10)
Little Common School, Bexhill-on-Sea

A Message To A Soldier
(Inspired by 'If' by Rudyard Kipling)

If you can keep your head when all about you,
When people are dying all around,
If you have that strength inside you,
You can urge yourself on with belief and determination,
If you have that disapproving voice,
Come, be brave, use your courage and hope for everyone.

If you can trust everyone when things go wrong,
Sometimes that trust is the key,
If you try to help everyone else,
Not just physically but mentally too,
They will get through this with you and your help,
If you are a lion,
Lead the pack,
Your confidence and faith will lead them through.

If you can remind yourself of your friends and family
Think *'I'm doing this for you!'*
If this doesn't help and kills you more
Be fearless, you will get through,
If you can focus on just that,
Storm through those barriers for your wealth and your country.

Cassie Matthews (10)
Little Common School, Bexhill-on-Sea

The Blitz

As the air raid sirens blast on everyone begins to run.
The dangerous doodlebugs destroy the Earth as they crash down.
The massive balls of destruction whistle on the ground.
The houses all around me die as they crash down in front of my eye.
The road is as wrecked as a blown-up project.
The rancid, repulsive, revolting smoke,
Squeezes my lungs as it floats around like a ghost.
The bullying of the fire makes me uneasy,
As I become really sneezy.
The little worlds of evil creep around until they blow up.
The sound of people crying in despair fills the air.
A bomb finally gets me although my spirit is still near.

Imogen Newport (11)
Little Common School, Bexhill-on-Sea

The Blitz

We walk down,
The street next door,
To look at the houses,
That aren't anymore.

'Keep on moving!'
The warden shouts,
Trying to keep all,
The people out.

Heaps of rubble,
Filling the street,
Miserable greetings,
With the people we meet.

Walls are swaying,
Like elegant dancers,
Performing wildly,
For those sorrowful glances.

Smoke is gliding,
Lifelessly along,
Fires are singing,
Their roaring song.

Chlöe Thompson (10)
Little Common School, Bexhill-on-Sea

World War Two

W orried mothers say their goodbyes
O nlookers weep and cry
R oaring sirens scream into the night
L uftwaffe approaches, louder and louder, a
D eathly silence floods the streets.

W ardens search the streets for light
A lamp is shining nice and bright
' R ight,' he shouts. 'Put out that light!'

T ogether families emerge from their shelters
W ondering what they will see this time
O ver and over the bombs are dropped . . .

Ethan Beech-Schubert
Little Common School, Bexhill-on-Sea

The Blitz

Yet another night has been
spent underground
As more bombs have
been found.

Wailing and weeping
They run for shelter
The smokey clouds fill the air,
Like the bombs falling in
the night-time sky
People looking at the
Rubble
Lurching towards them

The bomb came bouncing
through the
broken window.
The people
stared hopelessly
At the ruins of rubble
that scattered
On the floor.

Tiegan Caulfield (10)
Little Common School, Bexhill-on-Sea

Untitled

(Inspired by 'If' by Rudyard Kipling)

If you can fight when the world's against you.
Don't turn back when others need you.
If you can survive the trenches, the hunger, the loss.
But still give mercy to your enemies.
If you can have courage when others retreat.
Battle on no matter what happens.
Fight on for your family and friends for hours on end.

If you can believe in yourself and others.
Don't doubt yourself when something goes wrong.
Don't doubt others when they doubt themselves.
Don't give up and give them hope when they need it most.
If you can follow these rules then the war will be won.

Cameron Praill (11)
Little Common School, Bexhill-on-Sea

If

(Inspired by 'If' by Rudyard Kipling)

If you can keep your head when all about you,
Are losing theirs and blaming it on you,
If you can stay brave when things hurt you,
Don't fight back but think things through.

If you can dream, and make your dreams come true,
No matter what is stopping you,
If you can lose, but still pursue,
You'll find skills in yourself you never knew.

If you can believe when others doubt,
And carry on without dropping down,
If you can be tempted to find a way out,
Yet carry on, don't drag yourself down.

If you can be determined and stick with it,
But don't be too big-headed,
If you can think, *I won't quit*,
Then you, my son, can go ahead.

Sophia Rispoli (10)
Little Common School, Bexhill-on-Sea

If

(Inspired by 'If' by Rudyard Kipling)

If you can keep your head when all about you
Are losing wars, and your country's blaming it on you,
Then you can help people even when they doubt you.

If you can be a role model towards your countrymen
And if you are merciful, brave and strong.
If you are confident to speak aloud,
Then you can do anything that's in your mind.

If you can be inspirational, courageous and help your country,
And if you can say to your people,
'Never give up' and stick to that saying even when you're stuck.
If you have hope and faith in your country,
And if you have true trust in yourself.
And if you are proud then you are the best Prime Minister around.

Molly Kemp (10)
Little Common School, Bexhill-on-Sea

The Bloody End

Fire, fire in the night.
The blazing flames
Come into sight.

The whirly, twirly,
Misty air.
Slowly eases through
My hair.

The big black crow
Shoots through the sky
Then explodes before my eye.

Then the night is cold and bare
All I see is rubble there.

Will the bombers
Make amends?
Or will this be
The bloody end?

Luke Soden (10)
Little Common School, Bexhill-on-Sea

A Special Message
(Inspired by 'If' by Rudyard Kipling)

If you can keep your head when all about you
Are losing theirs and blaming it on you
If you have got the strength to fight for your country
Keep going, never stop - keep fighting and be brave.

If you can trust everyone around you
Though not yourself - keep telling yourself:
'I can do this' and don't fear anything.
If you have got anything to fight with keep it close by - stay focused.

If you can make your friends and family safe
If everybody else can put the bad behind them
And think about the good - then you can.

If everybody around you seems confident don't hesitate to start afresh
No one else will mind if you can do everything that has been said
Then you will feel as though you will be on top of the world.

Georgia Whiting (10)
Little Common School, Bexhill-on-Sea

World War 2

W hirring planes glide through the sky like a bloodthirsty owl searching for his prey.
O nly essentials will fit in the tiny suitcase, while the tight gas mask is hanging in the other hand.
R uins of destroyed houses lay on the floor, while smoke pollutes the air.
L ove spreads around the shelters as frightened families huddle underneath them, shaking in fear.
D evastated children cry as they see their huge house collapse on the cold, damp and muddy floor.
W orried fathers join the army, nervous they might die in the sloppy mud of the fields.
A ll the family gather round the radio anxiously waiting for news about the disastrous war.
R ound Europe thousands of frightened people sleep under the terrible leaking Anderson shelters.
2 close. People separate, wondering if they will meet each other again.

Michael Willard (11)
Little Common School, Bexhill-on-Sea

If You Can . . .
(Inspired by 'If' by Rudyard Kipling)

If you can keep your head when all about you
Are losing theirs and blaming it on you
If you can protect this magical, special
World but not let us get bombed
If you can take Germany down not let them win
You will make your country proud.

If you can lead the country to victory it would be outstanding
They will be ecstatic and trust you and have faith in you
If you can be brave and convince people that you are fine
They will help you through seeing the evacuees leave
If you can be strong when others can not
If you can help the ones that can't go on
Fight until you've won.

Shania Gray (11)
Little Common School, Bexhill-on-Sea

You Can Be Victorious

If you can sit in the trenches for hours on end,
Then you can fight for your country, family and friends,
You might find it hard and may want to drop,
But you have to keep going, just don't stop.

If the voice in your head is telling you wrong,
Just keep going all day long.
When the tough gets going the going gets tough,
Fight with all your might, never give up.

If you're tired and want something to eat,
Look around you, you're just surrounded by heat.
You can do it!
You can fight for your country, if you put your mind to it . . .

      You will be victorious!

Nicola Deans (11) & Rebecca Weston (10)
Little Common School, Bexhill-on-Sea

World War Two

W hat if there is someone watching us?
O ut of all the ordinary things in this world these
R ifles may be about to shoot us,
L and of ours might be about to blow up,
D ead people are lying everywhere - 'Help!'

W ar has started, it hasn't ended. Will it ever stop?
A t war we are. It's like it's never going to end,
R ight we are to stay alive but Hitler should die.

T wo wars there have been, all have killed
W e need more soldiers, win we will with more soldiers,
O n the 30th of April 1945 Hitler dies, we win!

Eddie Rumary (10)
Little Common School, Bexhill-on-Sea

The Blitz

Yet another night has
Been spent underground
As more bombs have been found.

I smell rancid, repulsive, revolting smoke
As it squeezes my lungs.
You can hear the crying and sniffing of mums
As you walk past them.

The walls of our house are wobbling
They might come down, forwards, backwards, all around
The ground is jumping up and down
As bombs are falling at 100s of miles an hour.

Scott Williams (10)
Little Common School, Bexhill-on-Sea

The Big, Bloody Blitz

Yet another night has been spent underground
As more bombs have been found.

I smell the rancid, revolting smoke as it
Squeezes my lungs.

Rocks are falling out of cracks in the ceiling,
As bombs bang on the outside world.

Smoke covering up a building,
Like a blanket covering a cold child at night.

A building falls with a crash,
As someone angrily throws a rock at the battered house.

Thomas Page (10)
Little Common School, Bexhill-on-Sea

World War 2

W alking down the dusty streets,
O n the ground, huge holes in the mud,
R aining ashes from the sky,
L ittle children start to cry,
D own in the cities, buildings burn.

W orried families waiting for dads,
A ll of the people are worried and mad,
R eady to fight, but all is sad.

2 many planes in the sky, hoping that they don't get shot down and die.

Lauren Harrod (10)
Little Common School, Bexhill-on-Sea

The Blitz

Yet another night has been spent underground.
As it squeezes my lungs
Bouncing bombs blast buildings to bits
White smoke looks like fluffy cotton
Wall moving gently in the darkness
People riding bikes
To get where cars can no longer go
The people see bits of the house
Where it has fallen down.

Zoe Wilson (11)
Little Common School, Bexhill-on-Sea

Bomb

As the bomb drops below
It shouts, 'Tally ho'
After the night
It's such a fright
As bits of bomb sizzle and crack
I feel like a mole
In a dark damp hole waiting to die
The big, bloody blitz
Has arrived.

Eric Davis (10)
Little Common School, Bexhill-on-Sea

If I Were A Bird

If I were a bird,
I would hear the
Gusty wind whistling in my ear.

If I were a bird,
I would feel the blazing heat of the sun,
Which is hotter than every star in the solar system put together.

If I were a bird,
I would see the horizon so colourful that it's
More magnificent than a sparkling rainbow.

If I were a bird,
I would taste the brilliant freshness of the
Crystal-clear raindrops.

If I were a bird,
I would smell the horrid oil from the sea
As I go like a jet over it whilst skimming the water with my feet.

If I were a bird,
I would hear the gentle flapping
Of my wings like a fan.

If I were a bird,
I would feel the cool breeze,
Against my soft feathers.

If I were a bird,
I would see the bright stars twinkling
In the jet-black sky.

If I were a bird,
I would taste the cold wind
Gushing like a wind machine into my mouth.

If I were a bird,
I would smell the sweet smell of
The beautiful blossom in spring.

Tom Haggis (10)
Maidenbower Junior School, Crawley

Once Upon A Rhyme

I found my sock beneath my bed.
'Where have you been all week?' I said.

'Hiding away,' the sock replied,
'Another day on your foot and I would have died.'

'Why would you make up such a lie
And why would you die you shy spy!'

Angel Foster (10)
Maidenbower Junior School, Crawley

Watermelon

'Be quiet and eat your dinner, stop arguing,' Mum says
'Be quiet and eat your dinner
Stop playing at the table, eat properly
Be quiet and eat your vegetables
Be quiet and eat your dinner'
I am getting a headache
'Be quiet and eat your dinner'
It's watermelon!
'Elbows off the table
Hold your knife and fork properly
Don't smash your knife and fork together
Be quiet and eat your dinner'
But I say, 'No!'
'Stop shouting at me and eat your dinner
Don't muck about at the table
Don't play your DSi at the table
Don't be rude to me ever again
Be quiet and eat your dinner
It's watermelon'
'Ok, I will try it'
Yummy, yummy, yummy in my tummy
'I like it Mum, thank you so much'
'Can't I leave now?'
'Yes!'
'Thank you for my dinner.'

Victoria Potter (7)
Patcham Junior School, Brighton

Curry

Be quiet and eat your dinner
Spicy food
Tickling on my tongue
Yummy
Yummy
In my tummy
Spicy food
Tickling on my tongue
Curry, curry
On my fork
Yummy, yummy
It's so, so scrummy
In my throat
In my belly
Yummy, yummy
Spicy
Spicy
Hot
Hot
Have a drink quickly
To get the taste out of my belly
Curry, curry
It's so spicy and hot
But I really like it a lot.

Lauren Shields (7)
Patcham Junior School, Brighton

Chicken Curry

Chicken curry
Chicken curry
First time we see it
We are desperate to eat it
It's my favourite
Chicken curry
Chicken curry
It looks like melted gold
Everyone wipes their forehead
Because it's so spicy and *hot!*

Marcus Taylor (7)
Patcham Junior School, Brighton

Beef

Beef, beef I hate it,
I cannot believe my dad eats it,
'I love you so much,' my sister says,
But I hate it,
Beef, beef, I hate it,
In my belly it is very smelly,
My mum tells me to eat my dinner,
It smells horrible,
Beef, beef, I hate it,
It has a horrible flavour,
Greasy and yucky,
Yuck! Yuck! Yuck!
Beef, beef, I hate it
Swish, swash,
Mucky,
Gooey,
Smelly,
Beef, beef, I hate it
Yuck! Yuck! Yuck!
My mum tells me to eat my dinner,
I cannot believe my dad eats it,
It smells horrible,
Beef, beef, I hate it,
Yuck! Yuck! Yuck!

Finlay Moore (8)
Patcham Junior School, Brighton

Pizza, Pizza

Crunchy, chewy, soft
Nice and cheesy
And tomatoey
Yum, yum in my tummy
My mum tells me, 'Don't play with your food'
Nice feeling in my tummy
My cousin munching away
Dropping pizza crumbs everywhere,
My dad stuffing his mouth
My dad eating it like a dog!

Bayley Dorrington (7)
Patcham Junior School, Brighton

Spag Bol

Yay! Yay!
My mum is cooking spag Bol
We are at the table
Oh no, my mum's put peas in there!
I try to dodge them
'Eat your greens!' says Mum
Mum gives me a drink
Slurp, slurp!
'Don't fill up on drink,' moans Mum!
I say, 'Done.'
'Eat more!' says Mum
I am the last one at the table
It looks squiggly!
I still have some
Chomp! Chomp! 'I am done,' I say
'Eat your greens!' says Mum
I get fed up!
So I finally eat my greens
'Where's pudding?' I say
'It is your bedtime now,' Mum says
'No pudding!' I moan
'Yes,' says Mum.

Poppy Wells (8)
Patcham Junior School, Brighton

Ice Cream!

Mini mountaintops on my spoon
Now,
Just watch the smooth, delicious ice cream
Melting,
Dripping
And dropping off the hard plastic spoon.

Mini mountaintops on my spoon
It's a real treat in our house,
Now,
It's melting
Dripping
And dropping off the hard plastic spoon.

Gracie-Ella Hassani (7)
Patcham Junior School, Brighton

Pizza

It's pizza for tea
Yummy, scrummy in my tummy
Slurping, burping
'Yum,' my mum says
It looks like a fat slice of cake
'Thank you for tea today,' I say
What is this?
It looks like an orange and yellow Frisbee
Great, excellent
Something special
Pizza
Pizza
I
Love
You
Pizza
Pizza
I
Love
You
I
Do.

Rachel Smith (7)
Patcham Junior School, Brighton

Spaghetti

Long sliding snakes
Slipping off my plate
Mum takes small amounts
Dad takes great big amounts
It sounds slurpy when you eat it
Slipping and sliding down my chin.

Slipping and sliding down my chin
Me and my brother hate the sauce
Oh no, it is down my shirt
What am I going to do?
Just tell her and finish my dinner
I have finished.

Cydney Crumbie (7)
Patcham Junior School, Brighton

Pizza!

Super tasty with long, stringy cheese.
A whole bit of pizza on the plate.
Red, fiery tomato sauce,
Long, stringy cheese, *mmmmmm*
Gotta get the biggest slice
I get some pizza, stuff it in my mouth
Yummy! I get another and another,
'Don't snatch,' says Mum.
Nice warm feeling of pizza in my belly.
I'm going to do the same with the others.
But I drop it!
'Go and change your top,' says Mum.
I go and change my top.
'Time for pudding,' says Mum.
'Get your elbows off the table,' says Dad.
In comes the pudding, more pizza.
'Get your elbows off the table,' says Mum.
I get some pizza.
I drop it - that really does it,
'Go upstairs and change your top!
Daniel Jones, that's the last time you have pizza at home!'

Daniel Jones (8)
Patcham Junior School, Brighton

The Fish And Chips

Scrummy, yummy in my tummy
Chewy, squishy on my plate
Slurpy, burpy in my mouth
Browny-white on the fish
Crispy lips smacking
Lovely crunch
It's so scrumptious and lush
And salty too
Lovely crunch
I am so lucky to have it
We're so excited
Lovely crunch
Lovely crunch!

Jessica Cobby (7)
Patcham Junior School, Brighton

Cookies

Yummy, yummy cookies
In my tummy cookies
Chocolatey, yum!
Chocolate chip and plain, yum!
Strawberry, yuck!
Honeycomb, yuck!
I want a cookie!
My mum says yes!
Only if I eat it at the table.
So I say I will and go into the kitchen.
But what do I see?
Oh no, Dad's got the last cookie!
So I go and tell my mum.
She says,
'There are some more cookies in the fridge
Especially for you!'
So I go to the kitchen
Wondering what flavour they are
And for goodness' sake!
My mum is mad!
I do not like the strawberry kind!

Anna Lawson (7)
Patcham Junior School, Brighton

Roast Dinner

Come on Fred
Come on Fred
What is it?
Looks like Santa Claus
I try it
Yuck
Tastes like a computer
Crunching, breathing
My sister's trying to blow up the table
Flying food
Now I know it's . . . roast dinner
'Argh!' I scream, then I faint
It's a Sunday.

Freddie Eriksson (8)
Patcham Junior School, Brighton

Sweets

I love sweets
Suck, suck, suck
I love sweets
Chew, chew, chew
They are minty
They are delicious
'Yum, yum, yum'
I love sweets
They are round
They are all lovely colours
Some are stripy too
But humbugs are the best
Oh yes
For me and you
Yum, yum, yum
I love sweets
But my mum says
'Don't eat too much
Or you'll be sick!'
'Spoilsport!'

Halle Vince (7)
Patcham Junior School, Brighton

The Peas

'Eat your dinner'
'No!'
'Why?'
'Because it's yuck!'
Small, round, green, yuck
Peas
Round, gooey, smelly, yuck
It's sliding down my throat
My mum is forcing me to eat it
Yuck
Eat
Yuck
Why?
I don't like *peas!*

Daisy Chilton (7)
Patcham Junior School, Brighton

Gammon And Egg

Crunch, crunch,
Chew, chew,
Goes the gammon,
Which is my food,
Swallow, swallow,
Yum, yum,
Goes the egg,
In my tum.
Come, come,
Gammon and egg,
You're gonna go,
In my head,
I don't like mustard,
Because it's bad,
All the yellow,
Makes me sad,
Delicious, ridiculous
Hideously nice,
Gammon and egg,
Definitely not rice.

Taylor Hale (8)
Patcham Junior School, Brighton

Ice Cream

Ice cream, ice cream in my head
Waiting for dessert
Tasty, creamy, chocolate, vanilla, strawberry
Pink
Yellow
Brown
Feeling
'Stanley! Ice cream!' shouts my mum.
I sprint down the stairs
There it is - I see ice cream in my bowl
I eat it all up
Lick
Lick
'Argghh!' Brain freeze!

Stanley Turner (7)
Patcham Junior School, Brighton

Pizza

Pizza, pizza
I love pizza
It's very yummy in my tummy
Eat it in a triangle
Red, yellow, brown
Pizza, pizza
I love pizza
Big, small pizza
Large, massive pizzas
Tiny, weeny pizzas
Pizza, pizza
I love pizza
Crunchy crust
Stringy cheese
I love pizza
Yum, yum, yum
Lip-smacking
At the dinner table
Pizza, pizza
I love pizza!

Freya Downs (8)
Patcham Junior School, Brighton

Pizza

We've got pizza!
Sizzling, bubbling, popping pizza
I can't wait to eat it.
We've got pizza!
Bite it!
Rip it!
Tear it!
We've got pizza!
Oh no! It's hanging down my chin.
Cheese, tomato.
Mmmm!
We've got pizza!
Melting in my mouth.
Oh it's all gone!

Mia Rahilly (7)
Patcham Junior School, Brighton

Sushi

Japanese
Taiwanese
Chinese sushi
I really like sushi
Yum, yum, yum!
Squish, gurgle and gulp
In my mouth
Yum, yum, yum!
My brother does not like it much
I can't believe he does not like it
I like it
It is the most lovely thing on Earth
Yum, yum, yum!
'Elbows off the table,' said Mum
'And keep your mouth shut.'
'Don't eat too much or you will get fat,' said Dad
'Don't nag me,' I said
I love sushi
Just give me more sushi
I love it.

Tom Satchwell (7)
Patcham Junior School, Brighton

Coca-Cola

Nice and bubbly in my tummy
Swishing down my throat
Fizzy bubbles make me burp
Dog's licking, I choke!
Bubbly circles pop out of my tummy
Mum tells me to drink from a cup
I get really upset
I stamp up to my room
Don't bother to kiss Mummy
You're just too mad about Mummy
Coca-Cola is my favourite drink
Nice and bubbly in my tummy
Swishing down my throat.

Alex Rathbone (7)
Patcham Junior School, Brighton

Spaghetti Bolognese

Yum, yum, yum
Spaghetti twirly, twirly
Always falling off my fork
Saucy spaghetti
Plain spaghetti
All kinds of spaghetti
Tastes like Heaven
Oh lovely spaghetti
I love you so much
I want you for tea every day
I asked my mum for spaghetti
She said, 'Yes, as long as you eat it at the table
And don't spill it.'
So I said, 'Yes!'
And ran off
But in two seconds I was back.
'You tricked me! There's no spaghetti at the table!
What's for dinner?'
'Stew.'
'Gross!'

Reece Irvine (7)
Patcham Junior School, Brighton

Pizza

Cheesy pizza
So scrunchy and crunchy
Even my mum agrees
That it's a scrunchy lunch
Take it into the garden
Eat it at your table

Cheesy pizza
So yummy and scrumptious
Oh it is hot, so hot
Eat it all, you must eat it all
It is really cheesy
Now I have finished it!

Luke Wakeford (7)
Patcham Junior School, Brighton

Chicken Pie

Hooray, it's dinner
And it's chicken pie
I cut my pie in two
And gooey chicken goes everywhere
It makes my mouth water like mad
Chomp, chomp, chomp goes my brother
'Don't eat with your mouth open,' says Mum
I take my first mouthful.

'Yummy,' I say, 'Yummy'
As it melts in my mouth
I've eaten the lot, except for one mouthful
I'm chewing so fast that I've got my mouth wide open
Ready to ask for more.

'Don't eat with your mouth open!' says Mum
As she gives me some more
And now when I look at it
The chicken and pastry
Looks like it's smiling at me!

Phoebe Megan Merrington (8)
Patcham Junior School, Brighton

Burger

Burger, burger
Lovely burger
Ketchup dripping down my T-shirt
Wipe, wipe
There, better
Oh no, my baby brother starts crying
Stop crying
In it goes - in my mouth. Yum, yum
Spicy, hot, cold
Any type of burger - I don't care
But here comes my big brother
He sits on his chair and starts shouting
'I hate burgers'
'Stop moaning,' says Mum
Maybe it's a bad day to have burgers.

Cooper Kryskiw (7)
Patcham Junior School, Brighton

Baby Ice Cream

Start,
Stick it on your head.
Freezing.
Make it into a hat.
Brrrrr.
Baby ice cream is yummy.

Catapult at Mummy.
He, he.
Throw it on the ceiling.
Ha, ha,
Aim at Daddy.
Perfect.
Baby ice cream is yummy.

Baby makes a mess.
Oops!
Kicks his mummy.
'Ouch!'
Baby ice cream is yummy.

Dominic Lock (8)
Patcham Junior School, Brighton

Pancake

We sit down to eat
There's a pancake
On the table
I snatch one
And eat it
I ask my mum
If I can have another one
And she says no
I ask her again
And she says no
But then she gives in
'Oh all right then
Have six slices.'
That is it
Now there's none left.

Oakley Mountney-James (7)
Patcham Junior School, Brighton

Eggs

I like eggs, every sort
There are fried eggs
The middle is runny
Oh no, I've dropped it.

I like eggs, every sort
There are boiled eggs
You have it in a solid cup
Oh no, I've dropped it.

I like eggs, every sort
There are cold eggs
They are nice
Oh no, I've dropped it.

I like eggs, every sort
Especially ones that are in omelettes
Some are Spanish
Oh no, I've dropped it
mmmm . . . nice.

Oscar Saunders (8)
Patcham Junior School, Brighton

Ice Cream

Ice cream is so yummy in my tummy
It slurps and squelches
Ice cream is so icy
Yummy, yummy in my tummy
It looks so delicious
So many different flavours
- Chocolate
- Strawberry
- Banana
- Toffee
- Vanilla

My favourite is chocolate!
Me and my family smile at each other
As we wipe the dripping ice cream from our chins
Yummy, yummy in my tummy
All finished!

Shauna Timoney (8)
Patcham Junior School, Brighton

Yuck, I Hate Cheese

'Here you are.'
'But Mum, I don't like Cheddar cheese'
Yuck, I hate cheese.

'Here you are.'
But Mum I don't like Marmite
'Cheese!'
'Yuck, I don't like cheese.'
'It smells like your feet.'
'I can hear evil cackles.'

'Here you are.'
'But Mum I don't like Margherita.'
'Cheese!'
'There are evil faces in holes
In holey cheese.'

'Right off to bed.'
'But Mum.'
'And no tea for you madam!'

Madeleine Fitzjohn-Scott (8)
Patcham Junior School, Brighton

Spaghetti

Yum, yum
Spaghetti
Meatballs are so stringy
Elbows off the table
Yum, yum
Spaghetti
My mum cooks spaghetti
Slithering, slipping, slithering
Down my throat
Here comes the spoon
Yum, yum
Spaghetti
Oh no, where has the
Spaghetti
Gone?
I know! It is in my tummy!

Poppy Tullett (8)
Patcham Junior School, Brighton

Pizza, Pizza

Pizza, pizza
I love you, I do
Yum, yum in my tummy
Ham, cheese, cold, hot, I love you, I do
Nice
Pizza, pizza,
Yum, yum
I love you
Crunching, munching
In my mouth
Hot, cold
I love you
It's great
My mum makes them
Pizza, I love you
Yum, yum
I love you
Yum in my tummy.

Aaron Finney (8)
Patcham Junior School, Brighton

Beef

I love you
You are so lovely
Beef, you are my best
Beef is dripping down my shirt
I love you beef, I really do
You are the best for me and you
If I could pick anything, it would be you
You are so scrummy
Beef you are deluxe
You are so delicious
Like chewy turkey
Your pinky, brown colour is the best ever
You are the scummiest ever
When you drip lots you are lovely
When I die my last food will be beef.

Sam Fowler (8)
Patcham Junior School, Brighton

Pizza, Pizza

Yummy pizza
With fiery red tomatoes
And
Long stringy cheese
The pepper was so bright
That it looked like someone had
Highlighted it
I wanted to eat the pizza before it was ever made
When it was made I took a slice
I blew it
Whoo, whoo
Put it in the mouth
Nice
Then my mum took a slice
Blew it
Whoo, whoo
Put it in her mouth
Nice.

Reuben Chilcott (7)
Patcham Junior School, Brighton

I Love Cookies

I love cookies
Hard ones
Soft ones
Especially chocolate chip!
Yummy and tasty
Round and precious
Like a golden coin
I love cookies
Especially chocolate chip!
Flat as a frisbee
Crunchy and munchy
Plain ones
Fruit ones
They're divine
Especially chocolate chip!

Jamie Nixon (7)
Patcham Junior School, Brighton

Sponge Cake

Sponge cake, sponge cake
    I love you, I do
Waiting for my sponge cake
    Bashing forks on the table
'I want my sponge cake,' says my little brother
'It's coming,' says Mum
'No, I want it now!' says my brother
'Ssssssshhhhh,' I say
'Yay, sponge cake,' says my brother
So my mum gives us it
I get my fork and I stab it
And scoff it down
With all the crumbs falling down my T-shirt
And we all go, 'Yum, yum, yum'
And we all say it's scrummy
And that night we dream for more
And the next day we have it again
And we say, 'Yum, yum, yum!'

Jude Kensall (8)
Patcham Junior School, Brighton

Yum Pizza

Yum, yum, lovely pizza
You look like a traffic light
Red, yellow or brown
Yum, yum, lovely pizza
Not freezing or medium
I love you, I do
'Stop shouting'
'Elbows off the table'
Eat it all
The tangy cheese
'Fantastic,' I say
Yum, yum, lovely pizza
'Be quiet, eat your dinner'
Crusty
'Yum,' you say.

Joseph Henty (8)
Patcham Junior School, Brighton

Pizza

Crunchy crust
Fiery red peppers
Yellowy cheese
Yum!
It is as good as Mum's
Spaghetti Bolognese
When we have pizza
For dinner
I jump up and down
But Mum always says,
'Eat your veg!'
When they aren't looking
I have some pizza
It's as good as Mum's
Spaghetti Bolognese
I can't get enough of it
Pizza, pizza is yummy!

Jude Johnston (7)
Patcham Junior School, Brighton

Tomato

'Eat your dinner.
If you don't you won't get any pudding.'
My little sister screaming.
My dad is sleeping.
My mum is baking.
And me? My name's Jasmine and I am waiting.
All this noise is making me scream.
'Be quiet,' I say.
Then Mum comes in with a tomato.
It's squishy and squashy.
I take a big bite and feel it slipping down my throat into my belly.
Bright as the sun.
I eat it all.
And now for pudding.
Yummy, yummy, yummy, yum in my tum.
The tomatoes look like moon squirters
Yum!

Jasmine Stantiford (8)
Patcham Junior School, Brighton

Burgers

Burgers, burgers
Skinny, thin burgers
Such a delicious, chewy taste
It sizzles and fizzles
We are drooling to eat it
Just can't wait
I just can't wait.
Burgers, burgers, chubby, fat burgers
Squelchy, squelchy, yummy burgers
Crunching in my mouth.
I just can't wait.
It's sizzling and fizzling in the pan
It's a delicacy to me.
I just can't wait.
It's crispy, chewy, yum, yum, yum!

Ewan Hook (7)
Patcham Junior School, Brighton

Chips

Chips, chips, glorious chips
So scrumptious
If they are close I will gobble them up
Chips, chips, glorious chips.

Chips, chips, glorious chips
Chips always look like yellow twigs
Soft chips, sometimes hard
Oh no, it's stuck in my throat!
Chips, chips, glorious chips.

Chips, chips, glorious chips
At the dinner table
Dad has an enormous amount
I have a small pile yet
Chips, chips, glorious chips!

Elvie Lawden (7)
Patcham Junior School, Brighton

Lasagne

Bubbly, round and greasy
Very bubbly and brown
My dad eats like a wobbly jelly
Look at me, I've got my elbows on the table!
It's nice and bubbly in my mouth
Now I'm shouting and screaming
I say, 'Hot, hot!'
I love lasagne
Delicious
In my belly it goes
Now I can leave the dinner table!
That was yummy!

Lucy Meighan (8)
Patcham Junior School, Brighton

Meatballs

I like it
My bowl
It's delicious
My favourite
Lovely red sauce
Not ketchup
Not blood
Not a red dress
Round in my mouth, soft and chewy
Bite in one go
I like it
My mum makes them.

Izzy Chitty (7)
Patcham Junior School, Brighton

Pizza

I like pizza
Scrumptious pizza
I cannot wait to eat it
Bite it
Rip it
Tear it
I like pizza
Oh no it's hanging across my mouth
Whoops I have made a mess
Oh no what is my mum going to say?
Oopsy daisy
I have eaten the entire lot . . .

Summer Pearson (8)
Patcham Junior School, Brighton

Crisps

Crisps, crisps, crisps
They are very crunchy
Crunchy, loud
Yummy, yummy in my tummy
I just can't get enough
Yummy, yummy in my tummy
Crisps, crisps
I just love them so much
Crispy, loud,
Yummy, yummy in my tummy
I love them so much
I just can't get enough.

Joel Hubbard (8)
Patcham Junior School, Brighton

Cheese

Cheese, cheese
I love cheese
I can't wait till I have my cheese
Cheese, cheese
I love cheese
Yummy, yummy, cheese in my tummy
I love cheese
I love cheese
I can't wait till I have my next cheese
All I can think about is cheese
I love cheese
I really want cheese now.

Liam Bennett (8)
Patcham Junior School, Brighton

Red Pizzas

Good or nasty.
Evil or yuck.
Yummy or delicious.
Cool, cool, cool.
It is red, evil tomatoes
And yellow, ugly cheese
And green, nasty pepper.
Spongy, spicy.
'Elbows off the table!'
'Eat your ugly vegetables!'
But I still like you.

Lily-Joy Bywaters (8)
Patcham Junior School, Brighton

Chips

Delicious
Yummy
Crunching
Munching
I love you, I do
Steaming, melting
Hot
'Elbows off the table!' says Mum
Yum, yum in my tum
Steaming chips on my lips
I love you, I do.

Lexy Bennett (7)
Patcham Junior School, Brighton

Pizza!

We sit down to eat pizza
Cheesy and spongy
Margherita flavour
Tomatoes look like red traffic lights
But I don't understand why my brother doesn't like it
I take five slices
It goes crunch in my mouth
It tastes marvellous
Sweet and yummy
But I don't understand
Why he doesn't eat as much as me!

Harvey Bostock (7)
Patcham Junior School, Brighton

Pizza

We got pizza
Sizzling and bubbling
Can't wait to eat it
Bite it
Rip it
Oh no, it's fallen down my chin!

Ben Yates (7)
Patcham Junior School, Brighton

At The Dinner Table

My brother throws food at me
It's horrible
It's like aliens at the dinner table
At my house
They make me eat things I don't like
It's horrible
My brother's screaming
And I'm refusing to eat my food
Because it's horrible
I have to stuff it in my mouth
It's horrible, trust me.

Lukas Bougas (8)
Patcham Junior School, Brighton

My Candyfloss

The best thing in the world is candyfloss
It looks like a fluffy, pink cloud
I love candyfloss
My mum brought it home for me
From a shop in the marina
When I got to the table
I started to eat
Delicious
I love it Mum, yum, yum, yum
And then I see the candyfloss,
      Is gone!

Gemma Rosam (7)
Patcham Junior School, Brighton

Cake

Yummy, tasty, delicious
It sometimes looks icy,
Sometimes we eat it at the dinner table
I go to bed when Mum and Dad tell me.
Then in the middle of the night when everyone is asleep except me,
I creep downstairs and eat some yummy, tasty, delicious cake.

Henry Simpson (7)
Patcham Junior School, Brighton

I Love Carrots

I love carrots
They are like
Orange darts
I love carrots
Raw and crunchy
Cooked and soft
Mum says eat with your knife and fork
But I just want to grab them
Handful of carrots
Snap! Munch!
I love carrots, yum, yum.

Thomas Owen (7)
Patcham Junior School, Brighton

Hot Chips

At dinner Mum brings chips in.
The chips are bright as a sun.
She puts some chips on my plate.
I get ketchup and I put it on my chips.
'That's enough ketchup,' says Mum
I want more ketchup.
I look at my lovely chips lying there in a little heap.
It makes me sad.
'Please can I have more ketchup?'
'No way, José!'

Hermione Barrey (7)
Patcham Junior School, Brighton

Lasagne

Layers of pasta spread out on my plate
Smooth, creamy and delicious with salad and balsamic vinegar
Crunchy lettuce in my mouth
'Stop stuffing your mouth,' said Mum
'I'm not,' I said
'Don't get too much salad,' said Mum
'Finished!' I said.

Faith Sampson (7)
Patcham Junior School, Brighton

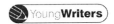

Pepperoni Pizza

Pizza, pizza
I love you, I do
Crunch, munch goes the pepperoni
Crunch goes the crust
The pepperoni slithers down my throat
'Yum, yum,' says my brother
Pizza, pizza, I love you, I do
Spicy
Hot
I love you, I do.

George Sumoreeah (8)
Patcham Junior School, Brighton

Chinese Food

Chicken balls crunch and are round
They roll around all over the ground
Oh no, it's on my shirt!
Rice is nice and skinny
And looks like tiny baby worms
Oh no, it's on my shirt!
Prawn crackers crunch and snap
And look like big white plates
Oh no, it's on my shirt!
Mmm, finished!

Gracie Pratt (7)
Patcham Junior School, Brighton

Pie

Pie, pie
It tastes crunchy on the top
And gooey on the bottom
It looks like an oval shape
At the table
I just want to eat it, in I go
When I eat it, it clicks down my throat
Pie, pie, it's so nice.

Findley Durrant (7)
Patcham Junior School, Brighton

Burgers

It's a burger
It's a burger
When I look at it
It sizzles like a sun
It bursts out burger bubbles
It burns on my tongue
Burger, burger, I love burgers
When my dad eats it he says,
'Look out!' The burger is hot
It's a burning burger.

Alfie Grove (8)
Patcham Junior School, Brighton

Pork Noodle Soup

I love pork noodle soup.
The way it slides around.
The silkiness of pork noodle soup
Makes me want a mound.
Ooh, I'm in love with the soup!

I love pork noodle soup.
Splashy when you drop it.
It's very nice without any spice.
So you should know where to plop it.

Fred Hoyle (8)
Patcham Junior School, Brighton

Crisps

Mmm, salty delights
Crunchy in my mouth
Mmm, salty delights
Broken and round
When I open the packet it sounds crackly
And it crackles and crunches
I love crisps, I love crisps
I love cheese and onion crisps
Mmm, salty delights.

Jessica Joseph (8)
Patcham Junior School, Brighton

We've Got Noodles

We've got noodles, noodles, beautiful, tasty
We've got noodles, wiggly, wiggly
Happy to eat
We've got noodles
It's dripping down your chin
We've got noodles
I can't help it, it's slipping down my chin
Yay! We've got noodles. We've got noodles!

Lewis Russell (7)
Patcham Junior School, Brighton

Pie

Pie, pie, wonderful pie
You can't resist pie
Pie is gooey, chewy, golden on the top
I love pie, yum, yum, pie in my tum
Sweet, sour or salty
Yum, yum, pie in my tum.
All finished now.

Abbie Bartlett (7)
Patcham Junior School, Brighton

Gliding

Gliding, fluttering,
In the light blue sky,
Shimmering, shining,
Soaring on high.

Flying, zooming,
Through a cloud,
Peaceful, quiet
Nothing loud.

I am the wind,
Standing tall,
My home is the sky,
Hear my call.

Madeleine Brockwell (9)
Plaistow & Kirdford Primary School, Plaistow

Majestic Mountain

My name is Mount Everest,
I'm taller than the rest.
My peak is a sparkling dagger that reaches into the sky,
Way up high,
Way up high,
My peak is a sparkling dagger that reaches into the sky way up high.

Startling sunsets light up my dull rocky body,
And casts a looming shadow over the world.
I like to suck up clumsy clouds as they float by,
Way up high,
Way up high,
I like to suck up clumsy clouds as they float by way up high.

Snow covers my body, like a warm cosy rug.
As noisy planes fly past I like to give them a nudge.
I see anxious climbers at the foot of me,
I wonder if they will conquer me.
I reward the strongest,
And send avalanches to the foolish
I can't run, I can't jump, all I can do is give climbers a bump.
But I still have room for sorrow,
As I have seen climbers collapse in their steps,
Falling down like they're giving me a hug.

I chat to K2 while sitting in a foggy gloom.
When climbers get to the top of me,
They stick a needle like flag in the head of me.
My feet are weighed down by tall, treacherous trees.
Other mountains bow down in front of me,
I wonder which one I'll have for tea.
Sometimes I see balloons go floating by,
Way up high,
Way up high,
I sometimes see balloons floating by way up high.
Then . . . *pop!*

This is the life,
It never really changes, does it?
I'm in Tibet, no Nepal,
Who cares, I'm on top of them all.

Leon White (10)
Plaistow & Kirdford Primary School, Plaistow

Volcano!

A volcano in the village,
A volcano in the village,
As quiet as can be,
As quiet as can be,
Watch out people,
Watch out people,
It's about to explode!

The volcano's getting bigger,
The volcano's getting bigger.
There's an earthquake happening,
There's an earthquake happening.
Watch out people,
Watch out people,
It's about to explode!

The volcano's getting smaller,
The volcano's getting smaller.
The volcano's getting hotter,
The volcano's getting hotter.
Watch out people,
Watch out people,
It's about to explode!

Spitting, spitting, magma falling down,
Spitting, spitting, magma falling down.
Popping, popping, spitting, spitting,
Popping, popping, spitting, spitting.
Finally the explosion ended!
Phew! Phew! Phew!
Look at all the wreckage.
'I'm so sorry,' mumbled the volcano.

Phoebe Mattison (9)
Plaistow & Kirdford Primary School, Plaistow

Volcanoes

Volcanoes are usually found,
Where the tectonic plates move around.
Beneath the Earth's crust . . .
Where the surface gets bust.
There, the sweltering hot liquid flows out,
Like a dead, leaking-with-blood trout.

Eruptions can last many weeks,
As the hot boiling gas slowly leaks.
Where the pressure is high,
The smoke fills the sky.
Ash clouds come toppling over,
A field full of one lonely clover.

The eruptions destroy many cities,
Putting them all to a pity.
They have all been wrecked,
And cannot be trekked.
So what's the point in them being there anyway.
Then a small flame of fire slowly sways.

Some of them are asleep,
Sitting there to weep.
Due to not demolishing enough,
They seem to be taking it quite rough.
But it doesn't matter because it will work out,
When the lava spills from their spout.

Samuel Vines (9)
Plaistow & Kirdford Primary School, Plaistow

Volcano

Once there was a volcano,
It was massive like a giant.
In the night the volcano rumbled,
Boom, bang, the lava came spitting out,
As fast as a bullet.
Lava is as hot as fire,
The lava comes running out to the village,
And demolishes it.

Nicholas Sutton (9)
Plaistow & Kirdford Primary School, Plaistow

The Fox And The Badger

Tonight, the fox goes hunting;
Tonight, badger goes hunting.
Together,
Together,
Together!

Tonight the fox hunts a rabbit family,
But the badger goes home,
How selfish!
How selfish!
How selfish!

Next is the feast,
But badger's a beast!
There will not be enough meat!

Badger comes back;
With oodles of rabbits,
Armfuls of vegetables,
And many little bugs!

The feast will go on!
The feast will go on!
Yell hundreds of hungry animals
Badger is not a beast!

Max Ragusa (9)
Plaistow & Kirdford Primary School, Plaistow

Dwoppy

I have a dog called Dwoppy,
His ears are very floppy.
I take him to the vet every week,
Which is on top of Penvile Peak.
I take him on a walk every day,
Where he likes to run and play.
My dog's very unique,
But sometimes he can really reek!
The vet says I should wash him every year,
Which I really fear.
I love my dog called Dwoppy.

Jared Allerton (10)
Plaistow & Kirdford Primary School, Plaistow

Trees

The average tree cannot see,
Neither can it talk.
It cannot hear the children cheer,
I've never seen one walk.

However, trees make homes for bees,
Their twigs make nests for birds.
I think each tree should always be
Spoke of by gentle words.

No tree looks like an animal looks,
But still they breathe fresh air,
Their bark is bumpy, all stiff and lumpy
Their leaves like human hair.

Overall trees are plants of peace
Harm they do not bring.
My message here is very clear
'Hurt no living thing!'

Kalamea Cropper (9)
Plaistow & Kirdford Primary School, Plaistow

My Garden

My garden sways in the wind
Like fluffy clouds in the sky
While I'm having pie.

My flowers are so healthy
They're eye-popping and bright.

My grass is as green as anything that's green
It blows in the wind rapidly.

My soil is the best you can get
It's as brown as a tree stump.

And a rainbow shines
Over the countryside.

Joseph Russell (9)
Plaistow & Kirdford Primary School, Plaistow

Flame

Flicker, flicker,
What's happening,
I seem to be losing my heat.

I know you would wonder,
How lightning and thunder,
Would make such a thing like me.

It's such a thing like me a flame,
Would be losing heat right now,
It's rather odd how cloud and fog,
Would drive me so insane.

Well now it's time for me to go,
I'll give you a good farewell,
It's not too bad being a flame,
It's just the wind, no don't
Open the . . .
Tss.

George Hardy (9)
Plaistow & Kirdford Primary School, Plaistow

Rocky Mountains

Rocky mountains, rocky mountains as far as I can see.
What next, just let me see.
When we got down the road to my very amazement I saw more mountains.
Off we go climbing up the mountains.
To the very top we must go.
Up, up, up, we go higher, higher, higher.
We go climbing to the top
Fast we go.
Come on, get a move on, we're nearly to the top.
Finally we have reached the top.
Raise the flag.
And back down we go.

Alex Jeffery (9)
Plaistow & Kirdford Primary School, Plaistow

Volcano Awakes

I am dormant, soon to awake
With a little help from an earthquake
My lethal lava seeps up to the top,
All the while I am getting more pressurised and hot,
The people live in fear,
Always listening out with an eager ear,
For when I might reappear,
And when I do they will surely know I am here.
The hot, sticky lava flows out of my heart,
Wrecking anything in its unfortunate path,
Spitting and bombarding the land with molten rock,
As more spurts out of my blown top.

Marcus Davies (9)
Plaistow & Kirdford Primary School, Plaistow

The Great Volcano

One day there was a volcano,
Dormant and calm.
Then the volcano started to rumble.
Ash started flying,
Rocks started cracking
And lava poured out like hot, sticky toffee.
Boom, rumble, smack go the rocks.
Eventually the volcano goes back to sleep,
But will it erupt again?
Nobody knows.

John Carter (10)
Plaistow & Kirdford Primary School, Plaistow

Dogs

Dogs like to bark but they're still lovely.
They jump up but it's ok.
Like my friends' dogs bark but they still love them.
My dog wakes me up.
But I'm ok with that and I still love her.

James Weston (10)
Plaistow & Kirdford Primary School, Plaistow

Flowers

Flowers are pretty,
Flowers are cute,
But not as cute as my
Dog, Bobby.

Flowers are nice,
Flowers are mice,
Apart from they don't squeak.

I like bluebells because they're pretty
And lots of insects would agree with me.

Elsie Wadey (10)
Plaistow & Kirdford Primary School, Plaistow

A Village On A Volcano

There once was a village on a volcano.
The villagers had frowns on their faces.
The cows ate all the flowers while wearing brown trousers.

The cunning chameleons were cunning but not enough,
For the volcano erupted.
Lava gushing out like there's no tomorrow,
The people ran away with the animals.

Connor Steer (9)
Plaistow & Kirdford Primary School, Plaistow

The Peaks Of Plaistow!

The peaks of Plaistow aren't very high,
In fact they don't even reach the sky.

They just popped up to say hello,
And now they've gone back down below.

Climbing up the mountain takes concentration,
But when you reach the top it's a celebration.

Alice Sheil (9)
Plaistow & Kirdford Primary School, Plaistow

Bob

There once was a boy called Bob
He had some food stuck in his gob
A slap on the back
And out it spat
All he did was sob.

Mollie-Anna Douglas (10)
Plaistow & Kirdford Primary School, Plaistow

Snow Leopard

I stopped dead in my tracks,
Even though a storm was brewing,
I stopped.

Then I saw a shadow in the distance.
I tried to sprint
But I was exhausted.

I collapsed!
I could feel the snow beating down on my neck,
Like tiny ice bullets.

I forced myself up, using all my strength.
The journey had been gruelling
And I was shattered.

A pair of red eyes emerged from the blizzard
Then the storm revealed a silhouetted body.

The eyes glared at me.
Circling me like prey until, he pounced.
The immaculate pattern showing.

I caught a vital glance.
It was a mountain predator.
A snow leopard.

Christian Martin (11)
Rocks Park Primary School, Uckfield

Through The Seasons

Badgers hibernating,
Snow falling to the ground as glittery as glass,
Winter birds sing in the trees,
This is winter.

Blossom sprouting from trees,
Animals coming out of hibernation,
Squirrels running around,
Little lambs as cute as a newborn baby,
This is spring.

Green leaves on the trees,
The sunset as beautiful as gold,
Beavers coming out of their dams,
The sun is shining down,
This is summer.

The leaves tumble down,
Animals collecting food for winter,
And finding habitats,
The lake as shiny as silver,
This is autumn.

Gregory Lewis Ledward (9)
Rocks Park Primary School, Uckfield

Snowflake And Star - Haikus

Snowflakes drifting down
In the winter night I fall
As white as can be.

I lead the wise men
To lead them to Bethlehem
To see the Lord, Christ.

I adore snowflakes
Shimmering down to the ground
As cold as can be.

I shimmer and glow
So high above the dull ground
So look out for me.

Louis Bissett (9)
Rocks Park Primary School, Uckfield

Snowflakes - Haikus

I fall from the sky
On the ground I do settle
White and cold I am.

White and crisp I am
I am a cold snow blanket
I fall from the sky.

I come at winter
I make a perfect Christmas
I fall on your nose.

I fall from the sky
I glisten as I fall cold
I settle freezing.

I am crisp and cold
I glisten in the sunshine
I am a snowman.

I am freezing cold
I'm a winter wonderland
I shine in the sun.

Robert Ross (10)
Rocks Park Primary School, Uckfield

My Pebble Poem

I am a crumbly, crunchy pebble.
When I travel to the sea
I grind, I break and I start
To feel trembly.

I am chunky, lumpy and bumpy
I'm as hard as a brick
But when I get weathered
I break down very quick.

When it rains and it's windy
I crash, bang into other pebbles
And turn into grains of sand at the bottom of the sea.
Now I'm so small some people can't even see me.

Emily Morrall (7)
Rocks Park Primary School, Uckfield

The Grand National

People crowded in
Wanting to see who was going to win.
Bets placed,
As they faced,
The biggest racecourse in the world.

One . . . Two . . . Three . . . bang.

Horses jumped,
Adrenaline pumped,
As the first fence appeared.

Lavender is the lead,
Followed by Semesters Mead.
Overtaken by Hurly Burly
Who is in front of He's A Guy.

They approach the finish line,
Summer's Wine,
Is in front,
Who will win? Everyone asks . . .

Zaveri Shah-Smith (10)
Rocks Park Primary School, Uckfield

Rocks

Rocks are big,
Rocks are strong,
Rocks are lumpy,
Bumpy and rumble.
Rocks go crash,
Rocks go bash.
Rumble and grumble all they do is tumble.
Rocks are tiny, smooth and rough.
Rocks make crystals and in them are fossils.
Rocks make buildings like houses and skyscrapers.
Crash, bang, boom!

Nathan Dowding (8)
Rocks Park Primary School, Uckfield

Rocks

I burn,
I expand,
I explode,
I lie.
I break,
I cool,
I vibrate,
I invade
The volume is
Like it's kaboooming up here.
That is how rocks are made.

Joshua Yexley (8)
Rocks Park Primary School, Uckfield

Trains

I'd rather be a train,
The great mighty beast.
Running up the hills,
Rushing through the tunnels,
Sleeping overnight, tucked up in his shed,
Ready for a new day, taking people all over the place.
From Brighton to London.

I wonder what it would be like,
With a great fire in your boiler,
Hearing people cheer.

Ben French (10)
Rocks Park Primary School, Uckfield

Violin

I'd rather be a string than a bow,
I'd rather be horse-haired than human,
I'd rather be singing than dancing,
I'd rather be playing a crotchet than a minim,
I'd rather be playing staccato than pizzicato,
I'd rather be in tune than out,
I'd rather be playing the melody than the bass.

Katie Nettleton (10)
Rocks Park Primary School, Uckfield

I'd Rather Be . . .

I'd rather be butter than bread,
I'd rather be a pencil than lead,
I'd rather be up than in bed,
I'd rather be a body than a head,
I'd rather use other words than said,
I'd rather be called Katie than Ted,
I'd rather starve than be fed,
I'd rather be alive than dead,
I'd rather have survived than bled,
I'd rather be black than red.

Katie Davies (10)
Rocks Park Primary School, Uckfield

Who Am I?

I am black like coal and white like snow.
I live in a hole underground.
I have stripes on my back like a zebra
And I come out of a hole in the dark night in Rocks Park School grounds.
I eat anything that is green.
When the trees rustle you can see black and white through the trees.
I have a body like an egg shape
And I am like a giant skunk.
Who am I?
A: A badger.

Maisie Morey (9)
Rocks Park Primary School, Uckfield

Rock Poem

I crack,
I smash,
I burn,
I crash,
I roll,
I weather away,
I bang,
I am a rock that is shaped like a block.

Alex Marsh (8)
Rocks Park Primary School, Uckfield

Volcano

When
I explode
I go boom, boom!
Everyone moves
Out of the city because
I will destroy it in a flash
My lava creeps like 10,000 snakes
About two hours later I stop
I turn very hard so you cannot break me
Because I'm igneous rock.

Callum Coe (8)
Rocks Park Primary School, Uckfield

Diamonds

I
Am
Very shiny and
Rare, and when you
Stare at me I glare.
You can find me
Underground safe
And sound in granite
Rock, there
I lay.

Bethany Hale (8)
Rocks Park Primary School, Uckfield

Pebble

I am a pebble
I bump down the rivers, look at me
I hoola-hoop down the sea
I bang side to side
I like to travel along
I am lumpy and bumpy
And I love it
Because I look so pretty in the sea.

Aimee Standing (7)
Rocks Park Primary School, Uckfield

Snowflakes - Haikus

I like to sink down
I adore the freezing cold
I'm white and tiny.

I fall from the sky
I am a white snow blanket
I make Christmas fun.

I make Christmas Day
I make a nice white Christmas
I'm symmetrical.

Joshua Stafford (9)
Rocks Park Primary School, Uckfield

What Is My Hole?

Mouse holes are small like a sharpener,
But fox holes are as big as windows.
Badger holes are just in-between though!

Black holes are the biggest of all, because they are in space,
But mine is just the right size,
What hole is mine?

Also I have a pink nose,
And two big floppy ears, like elephants,
I have a round body with two stubby feet, like turtles' feet.

Tommy Jay Taylor (9)
Rocks Park Primary School, Uckfield

Lava And Magma

Up, up, up, I go, whooooo.
I am orange and red
Going up, up, up.
I am as hot as the sun
Slush, I am going down, down, down,
I am so hot I can flatten anything.
I've come to the end of this life
Turning into rock.

Lorna Birkby (7)
Rocks Park Primary School, Uckfield

My Butterfly

My butterfly is as light as a feather.
My butterfly is as blue as a bluebell.
My butterfly is as small as my hand.
My butterfly drifts down like a snowflake.
My butterfly is as slow as a snail.
My butterfly is as sweet as a cupcake.
My butterfly is as special as a flower.
My butterfly.

Heidi Victoria Lane (8)
Rocks Park Primary School, Uckfield

Lava

Lava crashing
Rushing hotly
Melting, falling
Down, down, down
I am red, orange and yellow
I like to flatten, punch, crash
I'm flowing down, down, down
Keep away from me, I'm hot!

Louis Whitehead (7)
Rocks Park Primary School, Uckfield

My Lovely Bluebells

My bluebells are as blue as the sky,
My bluebells are as pretty as a butterfly,
My bluebells are as tall as a silver spoon,
My bluebells are as still as a spade,
My bluebells are as sweet as a cupcake,
My bluebells are as fun as a holiday,
My bluebells are as special as a gift.
Oh my bluebells.

Chloe Florence Costar (8)
Rocks Park Primary School, Uckfield

Magma

I bang
I boom
I crash
I am boiling
I am magma
I am red and orange
Hot, I cool, I burn
I am dangerous.

Thomas Nettleton (7)
Rocks Park Primary School, Uckfield

Tornado

Cyclone
Squall
Whirlwind
Capability
Cataclysmic
Piercing
Tornado!

Thomas Quinney
Rocks Park Primary School, Uckfield

Autumn Days

Autumn days where the leaves are crunchy like biscuits.
Autumn days where the leaves go brown like burnt food.
Autumn days where the animals collect things for the winter like we collect things.
Autumn days where the leaves fall off the trees like we jump on a trampoline.
Autumn is the smell of dead leaves.

Shane Harper (8)
Rocks Park Primary School, Uckfield

What Am I?

I have two round eyes
I live my life in a dark place,
I have an oval body,
I live in a cage,
As I listen, I hear the town,
The town is as busy as a bee,
But I have teeth like razors.

Luke Horne (9)
Rocks Park Primary School, Uckfield

Habitats

Habitats are huge holes, a nest and spiderwebs,
Crystal lakes and shimmering webs,
Trees like rough wood and mole hills like brown mud,
The huge trees like skyscrapers,
Nests like a wooden bowl and rabbit hole,
Very low down, dark and black
Owl branches high as a house.

Robbie William Thomas (9)
Rocks Park Primary School, Uckfield

What Am I?

I spend all my life in one place,
When I'm about ten I'm as heavy as an elephant,
Squirrels and woodpeckers live in me,
Sometimes I have a sort of house in me,
It's as big as four windows put together,
What am I?
A: A tree.

Alexander Beaven (8)
Rocks Park Primary School, Uckfield

My Creepy Spider

My creepy spider lurks in the corner of the bathroom
Watching me when I brush my teeth
Like a black spy camera that my sister is controlling.

My creepy spider is as scary as an eagle swooping down to catch his prey
My creepy spider looked different in the morning, tiny as a pea!
Maybe my creepy spider is not so creepy after all!

Katie Ruben (9)
Rocks Park Primary School, Uckfield

The Lake Of Doom

There's a pike lurking in the darkness of the lake,
As big as a dog,
There's a spider jumping about on the slimy lake,
A dragonfly zooming about like a plane,
But then a piranha comes leaping up and chomps
The dragonfly to death.

Michael Brimacombe (9)
Rocks Park Primary School, Uckfield

My Rock Poem

My rock is smooth, round and hard.
When rock melts it turns to lava.
If the lava cools down underground it makes crystals
Which shimmer and shine.
If you look very carefully you will find
Fantastic fossils and some are colossal.

Sam Brimacombe (7)
Rocks Park Primary School, Uckfield

The Big Dark Foxhole

Deep down in a hole like the darkest forest lurking is a fox.
Waiting for a rabbit to pounce on and kill.
His hole is very big and round, the fox is orange as sunset.
His tummy is white as snow.

Joseph Daniel Love (8)
Rocks Park Primary School, Uckfield

I'd Rather Be . . .

I'd rather be alive than dead
I'd rather be blue than red
I'd rather be Tyler than Fred
I'd rather be up than in bed
I'd rather be wood than lead
I'd rather be starved than fed.

Tyler Creech (11)
Rocks Park Primary School, Uckfield

Autumn Days

Autumn is like where the world gets covered in leaves,
Autumn is when the animals hibernate,
Autumn is like a big crisp with the leaves so crunchy,
Autumn is the smell of dead leaves,
Autumn is like the apples tumbling to the ground,
Autumn will be the same next year.

Leo Ferguson (9)
Rocks Park Primary School, Uckfield

My Dustbin

My dustbin stinks like a skunk.
My dustbin gets lived in by a skunk.
My dustbin gets emptied every day, unlike my bedroom.
My dustbin is my friend, unlike my parents.
My dustbin gets moved by the skunk.
My dustbin gets lived in by the odd fox.

Aarron Neal-Grigg
Rocks Park Primary School, Uckfield

My Pebble

My pebble is as
Small as a beetle
It can be smooth
And lumpy and
Ever so bumpy.

Saul Cannadine (7)
Rocks Park Primary School, Uckfield

A Dark Badger Hole

The badger hole is as dark as the night sky.
The badger hole is as muddy as my mountain bike
The badger hole is as lumpy and bumpy as the mountain
The hole is as messy as my house.
The badger's colours are the colour of the night sky.

Ethan Dadswell (8)
Rocks Park Primary School, Uckfield

The Holes In The Ground

The hole in the ground is the size of a door.
The hole in the tree is as big as a mole hole.
The hole in the leaf is as big as a caterpillar.
The hole in the ground is as big as a rat.
The hole in the grass is as big as a ball.

Scott O'Hara (9)
Rocks Park Primary School, Uckfield

Swishing Rocks

I am dashing like a dart so fast
Crash, bang, wobble.
I go down and then *boom!*
A hole, up I go out of the volcano.
It's tiring going up and down and around and around and around.

James Shannon (8)
Rocks Park Primary School, Uckfield

The Pond

The pond in the wood is as cold as an ice block.
The pond is a sparkly, frozen river.
The pond is like a gleaming world.
The pond is swirling around.
Swirling around in amongst there, is crab in the pond.

Catherine Waldock (9)
Rocks Park Primary School, Uckfield

Habitats Of Rabbits

Habitats are homes and where people live.
Some rabbit holes are enormous but most of them are small as usual.
But people see rabbit holes all the time,
People like rabbit holes because they put investigations on them.
But sometimes rocks tumble down on them like sticks.

Sully Willis-Gil (8)
Rocks Park Primary School, Uckfield

My Rat

My rat has a scaly long tail which makes my mum scream.
It has massive big eyes as black as a ball.
My rat is a little bit fat and very nasty.
I like my rat because I like its long whiskers.

Emma Bernice Leycester
Rocks Park Primary School, Uckfield

Winter

Winter is fun now
And winter is fun all the time
Snowy, cold, fun, ice
We love winter, it is nice.

Harry Beeney (9)
Rocks Park Primary School, Uckfield

Rock Poem

Round, round, round I go
Down, down, down
Falling over the ground.

Luca Baden (7)
Rocks Park Primary School, Uckfield

Snowflake - Haiku

I fall in the night
I make the ground white and cold
I make you shiver.

Ashley Geary (9)
Rocks Park Primary School, Uckfield

Snowflake - Haiku

Carried by the wind,
Cold as cold can be I lay,
On this winter night.

Ben Rowsell (10)
Rocks Park Primary School, Uckfield

Snowflakes - Haiku

White and crisp and fresh
Shining and sparkling tonight
Beautiful to me.

Beth Beasley (10)
Rocks Park Primary School, Uckfield

Snowflake - Haiku

Snowflakes in the sky.
And so bright as bright can be.
Snowflakes in the sky.

Andrew Stears (9)
Rocks Park Primary School, Uckfield

Snowflakes - Haiku

Floating in the air
Flying all around the world
Make the most of me!

Torben Rose (9)
Rocks Park Primary School, Uckfield

Star - Haiku

I glide and shimmer
I'm guiding the three wise men
On to Bethlehem.

Jules Dieleman (9)
Rocks Park Primary School, Uckfield

Snowflakes - Haiku

On the floor I lay
Footsteps on my white surface
I spread laughter too.

Alexandra White (10)
Rocks Park Primary School, Uckfield

Star - Haiku

I shine very bright,
    Santa sees me every night,
        Above a stable.

Freya Baldock
Rocks Park Primary School, Uckfield

Star - Haiku

Twinkling in the sky
As golden as gold can be
As bright as a light.

Benjamin Littmoden (10)
Rocks Park Primary School, Uckfield

Jesus Is Our Saviour

Jesus is our Saviour
And always gives us favour
And will help us with our behaviour
And gives us food with flavour.

Emily Konig (7)
St Wilfrid's CE Primary School, Haywards Heath

Stanley

Stanley was a cat,
He didn't like to eat rat,
All he wanted was to get a good present,
But he thought of getting a pheasant,
Finally he found some flowers,
But it took him hours,
Then he decided to make a cake,
He thought of putting on some flakes,
The cake was made out of mud,
But he fell and it made a bit of a thud,
That night he started having funny dreams,
But they had a bit of a theme,
The next morning he woke up,
And he told his brother and sisters, 'I need my cup,'
His mum's birthday had finally come,
Even though his mum had a big fat tum,
He still got her a gift,
So he still got to have a lift,
Mum loved her cake,
And for dinner she had a piece of steak,
She was sad in a way,
Because it was the end of the day!

Fay Hodson (10)
St Wilfrid's CE Primary School, Haywards Heath

Turtle

I have a giant turtle,
And she can glow bright purple.
She swims in the blue ocean,
Which is full of green potion.
She skims above the soft sand,
And pops up to view the land.
She dives down into the deep,
At nightfall she'll be asleep.
In the morning she awakes,
Watching as the sunlight breaks.
Looking for a bite to eat,
Wow, she finds a tasty treat . . .

Emma Pendry (9)
St Wilfrid's CE Primary School, Haywards Heath

Freddie, Our Cat!

Our cat lays around,
Asleep, snug and sound,
He lays on the rug,
All snug like a bug,
Freddie, our cat,
Brings in a rat,
He goes out the cat flap,
To go catch and snap,
He is as friendly as can be,
And his best friend's a flea,
His biscuits are a snack,
Then he cleans up his back,
He creeps like a mouse,
Up to the house,
Freddie likes to look at the sun,
He lies on his back having such fun,
Our cat Freddie.

Natasha Purchas & Sophie Bloomer (10)
St Wilfrid's CE Primary School, Haywards Heath

My Box!

My box can be a car and a boat.
But unfortunately it cannot float.
Should it get wet, which it hasn't yet.
It would sink in a blink of an eye.

My box can be a rocket ship and a secret den.
I can zoom to the moon
And visit the stars
And vroom back to Earth again.

In my box I can hide away.
Read my books, build my LEGO and play.
No one can ever find me
It's a great place to be.
When my mum calls, 'Finley'
To help her with jobs to do,
Like cleaning my room and flushing the loo.

Finley Rickard (10)
St Wilfrid's CE Primary School, Haywards Heath

The Chestnut Horse

Beautiful colours shining down from the sun,
Glistening on the wonderful chestnut. What fun!
Munching on the delicious emerald grass,
Playing with horse friends, having a good laugh,
Making a racket while eating fresh hay,
Snorting and kicking and saying 'Neigh, neigh'
Gazing at the bright blue skies,
While watching the buzzing, hungry flies,
Riding on his marvellous back,
Jumping over branches, flowers and sacks,
His blazing mane and furry coat,
He's so intelligent he can sail a boat!
But now his life is beginning to end
But don't worry, he'll rise to life again!

Gemma Batchelor (9)
St Wilfrid's CE Primary School, Haywards Heath

Lodge Hill

My poem is all about Lodge Hill,
And it can always fit the bill.
It is always full of leaves,
And has thousands and thousands of trees.
The food is extremely nice,
And is completely free of mice.
But before you go to bed,
Make sure not to bump your head.
When you wake up in the morning,
You might even hear people calling.
When you go out to play on the trees,
Be careful you don't fall and graze your knees.
It's always the top of my bill,
The truly fantastic Lodge Hill.

Erin Ross (10)
St Wilfrid's CE Primary School, Haywards Heath

Circus School

Mr Halford came in with a frown on his face,
Then he opened up his leather suitcase.
Springs came out flying, everywhere!
Balloons were soaring into the air!
His big sad frown became a grin,
Then the head teacher stumbled in!
He was the great ring master,
The strong PE teacher made a disaster!
The reception teachers wore leotards,
The caretaker did a trick with cards.
In danced Mrs Fleur cos,
The whole place had turned into a circus!

Freya Goodchild (8)
St Wilfrid's CE Primary School, Haywards Heath

The Tale Of The Dragon

Deep inside the fiery core,
An evil force awakes once more.
Plunging its wrath upon the Earth,
Thinking of revenge since its birth.
Amber eyes burn ever brighter,
Soon to grow to a frantic fighter.
Deafening beating of his wings,
It is greater than 500 kings.
Its glinting, glistening, gemstone hoard,
Means knights in armour are never bored.
But there's always a hero, braver and bolder,
So the dragon won't get any older.

Joe Goodchild (11)
St Wilfrid's CE Primary School, Haywards Heath

Waterfalls

Very quickly, fast drops of rain tumble down
Sharp cliffs of rock all at once,
Splash, pat, pitter-patter
Are the sounds it makes when it splatters onto tiny little leaves of wonder.
It's like a herd of elephants or rhinos racing to the chequered finish line.
Clouds of steam and the coldest splinters of water ever felt,
Puff up like camels' cheeks full of spit.
Beautiful bugs and dragonflies land on rocks of all hard kinds,
Buzzing in and out of the tower of water.
Who could have made such a peaceful creation?

Amber Tranter (9)
St Wilfrid's CE Primary School, Haywards Heath

My Friend The Squirrel

My friend Cyril
Is a grey and fluffy squirrel.

He climbs up trees
And dives in the leaves.

He loves his tasty berries
And his acorns he buries.

In the winter he likes to sleep
And in the spring he likes to take a peek.

Hayden Lunn (10)
St Wilfrid's CE Primary School, Haywards Heath

My Pet Eagle

My pet eagle
Is truly lethal
His claws are so sharp
They can rip through a carp
He can fly so fast
If you race him you will easily come last
He likes fish
It's his favourite dish
He isn't any old eagle, he's my pet eagle.

Adam Palmer (9)
St Wilfrid's CE Primary School, Haywards Heath

The River

Gushing currents float across the stream,
And water lilies of graceful sugar-pink and apple-green.
Fish splashing with scales of fiery gold,
Droplets of water spray are icy cold.
The glorious sound of water lapping up the bank
Once again it's Mother Nature who we should thank.
Though the clear water is cold enough to make you shiver,
I am truly grateful to witness the peacefulness of the river . . .

Isabelle Searle (11)
St Wilfrid's CE Primary School, Haywards Heath

Foxes

Foxes are cuddly and very red
They come out when we're in bed
They are very, very small,
I don't think they would like a pool
Their red shows best at night,
When the sky's not very bright.
There goes the friendly old worm
They don't come out at the winter term.

Patrick Baxter (9)
St Wilfrid's CE Primary School, Haywards Heath

A Baseball Poem

Stand on the podium with a bat
The bowler bowls and then you whack
If you hit it high you might get a home run
Or out of the park
If you hit it low you will get out
Single or double.

Luke Bates (8)
St Wilfrid's CE Primary School, Haywards Heath

Fluffy, The Killer Cat

In the morning breeze lays a ginger cat,
He is not thin, he is not fat,
His name is Fluffy, the killer cat.

He is an old woman's tabby cat in the daytime light,
And a vicious stalker when it comes to night,
His eyes turn from piercing yellow to demon red,
While the wrinkly old granny's still in bed.

A sleek black tiger prowling the street,
Nobody knows who he should meet.

Out come his severely sharp claws willing to fight,
He suddenly turns into a fearsome knight,
Teeth as sharp as razors, shining in the moonlight,
For anyone to look at, he is a merciless sight.

His eyes are blazing, his fur on end,
He stalks down the street and round the bend.
Into the garden where the windswept flowers grow,
Is his land every cat does know,
His coat as black as the night sky,
When a mouse scuttles by.

His feet kick the damp earth beneath,
He jumps at least 100 feet,
Powering like a superhero through the air,
The mouse gets a right old scare,
A blizzard whirring round the garden,
No excuse mes, not even a pardon.

The glowing sun comes up and he below a tree does stoop,
But not before he catches the loot,
There he sits eating it up,
Like a hungry, excited little pup.

By the cream and yellow patio,
There comes an extremely loud bellow,
'My pussy wussy kitty cat,
Where are you? Where are you sat?'
He turns into a loveable pussy once more,
As his owner comes out the door!

Alicia Drinkwater (10)
Stafford Junior School, Eastbourne

The Lazy Lie

There is a cat that roams around
Through the daylight in and out.
When there are people to see,
The cat is always on his knees.
When the guests go, it's coming up to night
Soon he will give you a nasty, ferocious bite!
Uh-oh, it's night!
Will he be the cat we know?
Will he be the cat we don't know?
The owner is ready to go out
For the night of her life.
She's gone, she's out,
What will happen now?
Bang! Bang! Boom! Crash! Crash!
He is the cat we don't know!
What will happen to this vicious beast?
He crashes, he turns, he runs around
All down the streets he has never found.
He runs as fast as a meat-eating cheetah
Looking for his prey.
Be aware - it might be you!
Let's hope he is home for midnight
He crashes, he turns, he runs back home.
He sprints like a pack of hungry hyenas
He is the wind blowing through the air,
The cat we know is back in town
His heart is soft and warm
Finally home, laying on the owner's velvet bed
He is a lovely cat
Apart from it's all just a . . .
Lazy lie!

Kimberly Irons (10)
Stafford Junior School, Eastbourne

The Shadow Cat

By now you should know to lock your doors,
And fortify your hen houses,
Because everybody knows,
Shadow Cat's on the loose.

From gutter to gutter,
The shadow appears,
Crawling through the waste,
But in a blink of an eye,
The shadow's gone,
He must have heard us coming.

For twenty years,
He hasn't been caught,
Not even by Sherlock Holmes,
We've only ever seen him once,
Up on the top of a hill.

His coat was dancing on the wild wind,
Eyes as fierce as a monster,
You might as well say,
He's a demon in feline form.

Now I think we should give in,
Let him roam the street,
Because we can't catch the Shadow Cat
Pouncing through the street,
Claiming a life a day.

Now I think we should give up
And let him lead this way.

Joshua Hackney-Ring (9)
Stafford Junior School, Eastbourne

Jo And Jane

Jo and Jane,
Must lack a brain.
Jo's ferocious,
A world class boxing champion.
Jane on the other paw.
Is curious,
At science college at five years old.

Both sleek,
Glossy and velvety,
Not at all like each other though,
One black,
One blue,
One day I'll rue,
That I told you.
They creep at night,
They'll scare you with their costumes,
In the day,
They're like angels.
Menacing and bizarre,
That's all they'll do,
From paw to paw,
Eating as fast as a cheetah.

When the golden waves in the sky,
Start to disappear,
Each cat will be upset,
All except . . .
Jo and Jane!

Arietty Powell (10)
Stafford Junior School, Eastbourne

The Dark Demon Cat

Sluggishly advancing on the street
Prowling vigorously in the squalid gutters
His eyes are as vicious as a gorilla
So hard to judge as me.
Mr Fetlix is his name,
One whisker, three claws,
And a cane,
He's a demon in feline form
With a disguise to hide the truth.
He has a shabby and tatty tail,
With a coat dancing in the wild wind,
Bristles are like minuscule mountains
And his legs as scatty as a beggar
Crossing the steep and straight buildings
And the feet with an evil frown,
The bulky monsters come by
With gruesome eyes of blazing fire.
The black ball of oil,
Rolling as rapid as a cheetah,
The musty coughs and sneezes,
Lay beyond the road across,
He is sly, snobby and a beast,
All day lying in the sewer,
Would anyone want to meet him?
Some cats decide not.

Oliver Message (10)
Stafford Junior School, Eastbourne

Varjak Paw

Varjak Paw was pouncing on the wall,
His heart was pounding like hailstones,
His hair smooth like grease on wood
His eyes cracked like shattered glass
His brain shattering like your mum's best china
His ears shaking like man in the Arctic
His lips twitching like a cricket in the night
His toes tingling like glass in your hair
His heart pounding like the beat of a drum.

Harry O'Neil Hughes (9)
Stafford Junior School, Eastbourne

The Cat Who Had A Dream

A cat was creeping upon a mouse
In a very sly soft motion
With evil aims and a venomous stare.
She's glossy with eyes like stars.
As black as coal she creeps steadily
With almost completely silent moves,
Sure to give the mouse a startle.
She leaps and pounces at the mouse,
She slides one soft paw on the mouse
And starts scratching at the fur.
A brown ball of fluff lays noiseless on the floor.
Suddenly the cat awakes
While licking at her paw.
Only if that weren't a dream
She would have had a feast.
She lays upon a pillow as golden as the sun.
She's very respectable with a feline shape.
I could say she's competitive.
With claws as sharp as knives
You wouldn't want to mess with her.
She creeps outside and catches a mouse,
Her dream has come true at last.
The cat who had a dream.

Kiera-Mai Capon (9)
Stafford Junior School, Eastbourne

Varjak Paw

Varjak's heart pounding like an elephant stomping,
His brain is a mixed up dictionary,
His hair is as scruffy as an old teddy,
His eyes are brighter than the sun,
His tail is like a skipping rope,
His ears are twitching like a ticking clock,
He is feeling so terrified it's hard to believe,
A blast of wind could knock him over,
His shaking is so strong it could knock over a wall,
His grandfather is as strong as a gorilla,
Varjak's whiskers are steel!

Danielle Morgan (9)
Stafford Junior School, Eastbourne

There Is A Mystery Cat

There is a mystery cat
He is a bat
His eyes glow red
His tail is straight up
There is a mystery cat.

There is a mystery cat
His prey is as slow as a human
And he's as fast as a Bugatti Veyron
There is a mystery cat.

There is a mystery cat
With a red hat and a blue body
With a tail as long as a lizard
There is a mystery cat.

There is a mystery cat
His body is as sharp as a dinosaur's tooth
His longest strike is as long as a street
There is a mystery cat.

There is a mystery cat
His tail is as monstrous as a dog
His back is the best in town
There is a mystery cat.

Adam Milsom Smith (10)
Stafford Junior School, Eastbourne

Varjak Paw

Varjak is striding on the wall,
His brain is a ticking clock,
His hairs are pointed pins,
His tail is flicking like a whip,
His heart is pounding up his throat,
His eyes are as round as a disco ball,
His eyes twitching like a ticking grasshopper,
His eyelashes flickering like a broken light,
His brain shouting, 'Run away from that monster,'
His legs shaking like an earthquake,
His heart hitting his chest like a herd of elephants.

George Cooper (10)
Stafford Junior School, Eastbourne

Fluffy The Killer Cat

In the summer breeze lays a ginger cat.
He is not thin, he is not fat.
His name is Fluffy, the killer cat.
He is an old woman's cat
In the daytime light.
And a vicious demon when it comes to night.
Eyes turning from yellow to ruby-red.
While the old woman's still in bed.
A sleek black tiger crawling the streets.
Nobody knows who he should meet.
Drawing his claws, willing to fight.
Suddenly turns into the black night.
Teeth as sharp as razors.
Gleaming in the moonlight.
For anyone to look at,
He is a fearsome sight.
Eyes blazing,
Fur on end.
He rampages round the street
And down the bend.
He turns into a pussy once more
As his owner steps out the door.

James Bown & Connor Summerfield (10)
Stafford Junior School, Eastbourne

Greedy, Greedy Cat

Sleepy, lazy, tired, greedy
You all know the sneaky cat,
He wanders in the night
He sleeps in the day
You all know the sneaky cat
He's sneaky, he's silent
He never makes a noise
His eyes as red as the sunset.
Glowing in the dark as they always do.
He's sneaky, he's silent, and he never makes a noise.
You all know the sneaky cat.
Boom!

Amy Clarke (9)
Stafford Junior School, Eastbourne

Varjak Paw

Varjak, amazed, up on the wall,
His nails cling in amazement.
His eyes as wide as can be,
Tail swings back and forth,
Up in the sky birds fly like never before,
His heart is a ticking clock,
Terrified of all the noise,
Other cats with owners,
His eyes as bright as the sun,
The world is as loud as a lion's roar,
As brainy as a calculator,
Like never before,
The wind sings,
Paws cling onto the wall, purring loudly,
Perching deeply into the wall,
When he looks back it is dark,
When he looks forward it is bright,
Which one to choose from,
Which one is right?

Ellie Mizen (9)
Stafford Junior School, Eastbourne

The Majestic, Mysterious Cat

Cats pouncing like a majestic kangaroo into the open space of the world.
Eyes like balls of fire.
Trees swaying beautifully on the trembling world.
Cars roaring across the road like a hyena catching its prey.
He's a soft ball of fur creeping into
Lots of broken-down fences.
The golden sunrise glints into his mustard eyes.
The wind blowing its proud force crashing into him like lightning.
No food, just broken bones
And muddy sandwiches surrounding his path.
His swaying tail is like a monkey swinging on vines.
His prowl is like a lion's roar.
Survival, strength and courage are all that matters in this world.
When it is dark all you can see are his glittering golden eyes,
Glaring at you with ferocity.

Aaron Clarke (10)
Stafford Junior School, Eastbourne

Varjak Paw

Varjak leans over, his paws like a flapping bird
His ears shaking like a man being rocked
His tummy rattling like a baby rattle in agony
Varjak's blood rushes like a crocodile snapping
Varjak's head twitching like a person having a fit.

His head turns like an owl flapping his wings
His tail flickering like a baby dying at a hospital
Varjak's knees shiver like a weak person
Varjak staring with his big eyes, his nose squawking
His mouth is open like a dog's barking mouth.

His tongue licking like a cat trying to lick the mouse
His face shuttering like a fetching dog
A man trying to get a cat out of a cage
The cat has an open mind like a beast.

His heart pounding like a pen waiting to sing out
Varjak sits like a broken stone, his bones waiting
His insides waiting to make cupcakes like a slow cooker.

Jasmine Loats (10)
Stafford Junior School, Eastbourne

The Football

I'm lost.
Sad.
At the edge of a field.
Twiggy bush.
For three sunny days.
Can't wait till I'm found.
People rushing by . . . Fast!
Will someone see a ball? Me!
Boy with brown hair, crawling through the thorns.
At his house,
Play with me!
Do I want to go to the park? Yes!
Ten boys, all ten.
Scared! Kicked! Penalty! Goal!
Cheers! Happy!
I'm found!

Samuel Eade (9)
Stafford Junior School, Eastbourne

Varjak Paw Poem

Whatever he hears, says or miaows
He always has a heart,
He prays to God every night of the week,
Hopes things will go right.
He never cries
Never sheds a tear, only when his fur's on end.
He has yellow eyes like the big, bold sun.
His paws are like shoe polish,
How he has a heart of gold, he knows,
It's just the luck he cherishes,
He sits on the wall,
The wall that's brown,
Brown as mud where someone's died.
Like a funeral bed.
People wishing they could be alive,
So every night he curls up like a chinchilla
Not in a funeral bed, in a wooden basket.
Goodnight, sleep tight.

Dennie Bull (10)
Stafford Junior School, Eastbourne

Facebook Boy - Addicted

I am 15.
I live on Nevil Road, Bexhill
(He has a hundred friends on Facebook.)

I think that I am a comedian.
I am short.
(He has a hundred friends on Facebook.)

I have black hair, short, spiky and gelled with pink highlights.
(He has a hundred friends on Facebook.)

I have to wear round glasses that make me look weird!
I am grumpy!
(He has a hundred friends on Facebook.)

I like Xbox 360 games.
My favourite subject at school is home time.
(He has a hundred friends on Facebook . . . but nobody likes him.)

Aidan Ripley (10)
Stafford Junior School, Eastbourne

Varjak Paw

Varjak advances into open space,
His orange eyes are balls of fire,
His prowl is a Lamborghini's engine,
Sunrise projects like shaded sound waves.

Fur as soft as a velvet pillow,
Buildings stand tall like steep, brick mountains,
Trees swishing like hands waving,
The wind whispers, 'Hurry up, hurry up.'

Thoughts fill his mind like sweets in a piñata
He can't get them out without a helping hand,
His heart is a ticking clock, time running out,
He has to act fast or Elder Paw is ended.

The black cats are so mean and large,
Varjak's shadow casts across the wall,
Thunderous roars echo in the distance,
It's getting louder, is this the dogs?

Jevan Luke Cousins (9)
Stafford Junior School, Eastbourne

The Mystery Cat

There is a mystery cat,
Who lives like a bat.
His tongue is like a snake,
He eats and eats all day long with his horrid aunt.
He never listens to his mother or father.
His face is a glowing black hole.
This cat is indeed very strange, every night he disappears
He is invisible.
This cat is a ball of fluff,
He disappears out the door.
He is as stealthy as a fox.
He comes back with muddy footprints
His mother and father think he is quite strange.
He comes back with different crafts but he hides them.
His fur is a bird.
I wonder who he is.
But we will find out won't we . . .

Ryan Winters (9)
Stafford Junior School, Eastbourne

The Mysterious Cat

She is a sly, sneaky fox,
Slipping through the town,
Breaking into buildings,
Fracturing glass as she goes.

Claws like a skunk's tooth,
Help her to climb so high.
Eyes are golden brown,
Coat is the night sky.

The wind screams at her to stop,
Trees try to scare her away,
Walls as proud as they can be,
Are just a pile of twigs to her.

Then eyes which can see anything,
Claws homing into the prey.
Invisible to everyone but her,
For she is the feline devil.

Jacob Norris (10)
Stafford Junior School, Eastbourne

Varjak Paw

Varjak, digging his claws into the tarmac,
Scared and surprised,
His hair sticking up on end, like a million twigs,
His heart racing faster than ever before,
His brain shouting, 'What is going to happen next?'
Closer and closer,
Wider and wider,
The monster is coming,
His eyes are giant footballs,
His mouth dropping like a ferocious, hungry tiger,
Ears twitching back and forth,
A blasting of bitterly cold wind in Varjak's face,
In the glaring sky,
Pictures of poor, abandoned grandfather,
Still, extremely worried,
His body losing strength to walk,
Miaow.

Valentina Pescatore (9)
Stafford Junior School, Eastbourne

The Mysterious Cat

The mystery cat, he's cheeky,
Sneaky and stealthy
When something breaks the mystery cat is gone
But in the day he's cute and cuddly
Playing around with his foul breathing monster
Keeping his identity secret
But in the night he stands tall with his ruby-red eyes
And proud, snooping down
Shaking gutters glittering like eyes
Leaving no prints like a magic cat
On the grass or on the ground
But when they go out and look for
The demon feline in form
He's nowhere to be seen
But in plain sight.

Jason Grave-Dawson (10)
Stafford Junior School, Eastbourne

Varjak Paw

Varjak viciously dashed up the wall like a speeding V5 rocket.
His heart was a ferocious thunderstorm.
His tail was flicking like bugs' wings flapping.
Varjak's orange eyes were the luminous orange sky.
His big pupils were growing bigger as the time carried on.
His hair was sticking up like razor-sharp blades.
He could hear monsters roaring, people making funny noises.
He could feel the air brushing against his furry tail.
'Did I do the right thing? Should I have stayed?'
His heart was pounding to find a dog.
'Were those monsters dogs? I'm not sure,' mumbled his mind.
He could see his blurry reflection in a gigantic puddle.
Was this tunnel, countryside or cave, ever going to tell him the way . . .
Or show him to the dogs, so he could help Elder Paw?
He was searching for a dog like a furious, ferocious, fire phoenix.

Imam Houssein Barrientos (10)
Stafford Junior School, Eastbourne

Varjak Paw

Varjak's orange eyes stared into the sky,
His wet nose wrinkled in the sunlight,
Yet the wall was so cold.

He could see into the horizon
Grass as soft as a feathered pillow,
But yet it seemed so dull.

Varjak stared at the little butterflies,
They fluttered around like birds,
Varjak just sat and stared.

His paws were shaking,
His heart was thumping,
His mind was spinning.

Rachel Marley (9)
Stafford Junior School, Eastbourne

Varjak Paw

It looks like nothing he has ever seen,
It looks like nowhere he has ever been,
His heart pounding,
His brain ticking,
His eyes are fearful,
His paws are frozen.
The cold air is flying through his thick black fur
As his tail is whipping against the stone wall.
Varjak's whiskers are icicles.
His mind is telling him to go back but he has to keep going.
He can see the dogs, their massive teeth.
His paws are frozen lakes
But he knows he must go and find a dog.

Helena Jeffery (9)
Stafford Junior School, Eastbourne

Varjak Paw

The wind swaying slowly in his eyes,
His yellow eyes looking in different directions everytime,
Lightning bolts shooting to the ground
And making Varjak jump,
So his fur is sticking up on end,
He's confused, What should he do?
Stay or go?
And go on an adventure,
His choice, don't know what to do.
The new world's wind is blowing in his face,
He can see trees swaying and cats in alleyways.
The wind is getting stronger and stronger.
'I want to go back to Elder Paw.'

Grace Maynard (10)
Stafford Junior School, Eastbourne

Poem Of Varjak Paw

Varjak's eyes are as orange as a fire flame
His brain is confused like a person knocking its head on a tree
Varjak's hair stands up on end like his brother Julius,
The meanie!
Varjak perches on the wall scared to death
His body shaking like a bit of thunder has just struck him
His tail flickering mad, scraping the wall
(Bet that hurts)
The headlights are flickering in his eyesight
As fast as a cheetah running
Mouth wide open with a surprised look on his face
Elder Paw is yelping as a person who has just been stabbed.

Kirsty Sammes (9)
Stafford Junior School, Eastbourne

Who Is It?

As loud as a storm
As soft as a pillow
As fierce as a tiger
As bright as the sun
As big as a polar bear
Its whiskers are as sharp as a sword
Its tail as quick as a car
Its fur is as fluffy as a teddy bear
Its mane is as orange as a carrot
Its teeth are so dirty, as dirty as mud
Its mouth is very hungry
Who is it?

Emily Tucknott (10)
Stafford Junior School, Eastbourne

The Sad Life Of A Street Cat

She strolled along in the wide open space,
The shops glared at her with their blinding lights.
Her crumpled-up fur coat sticky with mud,
Rippled in the Arctic midnight air,
All she could pick up was,
The foul scent of littered food,
Making her feel queasy,
But also making her starve,
Her paws went limp as if she had broken them,
She would do anything for a sliver of food,
Her tail fell down behind her body as she froze,
Then she fell to the ground like a wilting flower.

Jasmine Ward (10)
Stafford Junior School, Eastbourne

Varjak Paw Poem

Varjak's ears twitching like a rabbit,
His eyes as wide as a computer screen,
His shivers as cold as ice,
His mouth open like an unlocked vault,
His brain whispering to follow the steps of Jalal,
His footsteps moving to the edge of the wall,
His heart throbbing like an angry bull,
His tail standing up on end,
His chest as slouchy as a panda,
His back hair standing up on end,
His head as confused as a fish,
His eyes as orange as an orange.

Sapphira Nicole Christoforou (9)
Stafford Junior School, Eastbourne

Varjak Paw

Varjak stands on the wall, with a graceful look
His eyes are like a soft ball of grass
His fur stands on his body, like the boy next to me
The pointing, furry ears which shriek to your cuddly head
His brain starts to wonder what the others are talking about
They are like a pack of hyenas
He starts to lick his lips as fast as an F16 reaching its top speed
Varjak pounces from the wall, like a hunting lion
His nose twitches up and down like a game of ping pong
His eyes light up as the smell of cat food drifts through his nose
But his body starts to drop, the others have already eaten.

Ernie Pownall (10)
Stafford Junior School, Eastbourne

The Way Of The Lion

He's as tough as a brick
As strong as a bear
As large as a fridge
Roar! Roar! The noise of the beast.

As cunning as a fox
As furry as a panda
The beast is called a lion.

Lion, lion, that's the name
The lion is big
The lion is fearsome . . .

Scott Jeffery (9)
Stafford Junior School, Eastbourne

The Mystery Cat!

He pounces like a skimming stone,
He is an angry cheetah,
The mystery cat is no ordinary cat,
He likes to explore the night,
When he's in town roaming around,
He likes to give people a fright,
The mystery cat has a violent soul,
Which nobody dares to seek,
Don't ever come across him,
For he will make you shriek!

Luke Lawrence (10)
Stafford Junior School, Eastbourne

Varjak Paw

His heart pounding like a ferocious thunderstorm.
His feet slipping, losing strength as the cars came closer.
His eyes scanning the road like a radar.
His bones decaying as he walked along in terror.
His ears twitching intensely as the shadows slowly crept their way past.
His heart being filled with cold blood
As he walked further away from Elder Paw.

Jamie Rennie (10)
Stafford Junior School, Eastbourne

The Troublemakers

Once there were two young cats
Their names were Bella and Ben
Lovely in the daytime
But trouble in the night
They would pounce and play all through the day
But in the night they changed their ways
All through the night they would chase the mice
And eat the spice
By day they acted all innocent like a dog
Who's ripped the curtains.

Mollie Macdonald (9)
Stafford Junior School, Eastbourne

Varjak Paw

Varjak was as terrified
As a monkey's first jump,
His eyes like a crackling fire,
'I'm out,' he said,
The wind howling through his ears,
His fur flying through the air,
The house as big as a wall,
His eyes popped out of his head,
He looked back, shrieked in terror
Calling back, 'I'll save you Grandad!'

Francesca Tann (10)
Stafford Junior School, Eastbourne

Varjak

Varjak - he stands on the wall.
The wind talks to Varjak. 'Varjak!' says the wind, he can see anything.
The sky is red, pink, blue and green. It is a paint pot.
Varjak looks behind him. Elder Paw is dead like a toy.
Varjak shivers in the cold breeze.
The next thing he is slipping.
Then he runs as fast as a Ferrari Enzo, in the swift wind.
Varjak jumps like an athlete and makes it.

Oliver Thom (9)
Stafford Junior School, Eastbourne

The Mystery Cat

Cats pounce into the open space like a majestic kangaroo.
They fight for their prey as fast as a Bugatti Veyron.
Cats' eyes are shaped like a huge bubblegum.
Their tongues are as thorny as concrete.
His tail swings from side to side like a monkey on vines.
They are goblins with scorching black fur.
Cats prowl like a lion roaring.
He is as sly as a ginger fox.
His name is Tootie.

Daniel James Carter (10)
Stafford Junior School, Eastbourne

The Dancing Cat

The dancing cat prances and twirls,
She leaps like an angry cheetah,
Her lips are as red, as a rose.

She twirls and whirls every day,
Her whiskers are as sharp as a needle,
She has no claws,
And no jaws,
Her tutu is as frilly as a little girl's hair.

Isabella Davy (9)
Stafford Junior School, Eastbourne

Samba The Street Cat

She spends her nights,
Wandering past the dark and dismal shops
Her black, crumpled fur coat,
Ripples in the midnight air,
All she can smell is the scent of littered food,
The minute she hears a creak or a crack,
She has her claws as sharp as a razor,
Back on the streets again for a new dawn.

Rebecca Tyhurst (10)
Stafford Junior School, Eastbourne

The Mystery Cat

The mystery cat is a savage feline,
Who likes to explore the night,
His eyes are as red as rubies,
He likes to give people a fright.
The mystery cat has a violent soul,
Which nobody dares to seek,
He has legs like coiled springs
And he will make you shriek.

Joshua Luis Da Silva (10)
Stafford Junior School, Eastbourne

The Angry Cat

There was a juvenile cat
But he was no ordinary cat.
Like a magic moggie only when
He was on a rampage
He was a bulldozer knocking everybody in his way
His eyes were like balls of flaming fire.
His fur was like the night sky.

Joshua Prysor-Jones (10)
Stafford Junior School, Eastbourne

Dangerous Marvin

Watch out for the mighty dangerous Marvin,
Don't go near him otherwise you will be scratched to death.
He's the most violent cat in Liverpool,
Be careful, he's coming to you
Because no one liked him where he lived,
Beware if you're out, he's coming about.
He's a bloodthirsty wolf, so watch out.

Giorgia Lauren Olding (10)
Stafford Junior School, Eastbourne

Universe

Big and dark,
Eternally large,
Planets and stars,
Pluto, Venus and Mars,
Orion's Belt,
Libra and Capricorn,
Stared at for hundreds of years,
They are very worn,
Leo, Taurus, Aries too,
And little old Pluto is actually blue!
Big and dark,
Eternally large,
Planets and stars,
Pluto, Venus and Mars,
Asteroids and meteors,
Always looking queer,
Comets and shooting stars,
Flying through the atmosphere,
Big and dark,
Eternally large,
Planets and stars,
Pluto, Venus and Mars.

Frances Romain (11)
The Globe Primary School, Lancing

The Whirlpool Monster

The whirlpool monster
The whirlpool monster
Six gruesome heads
Six gruesome heads
Crunch, crunch, crunch!
The six gruesome heads
Gruesome monster
Gruesome monster
Crunch, crunch, crunch,
Crunch, oh, ow, monster,
Monster,
Angry monster!

Emma Downs & Rebecca Collins (8)
The Globe Primary School, Lancing

A Fallen Star

A star fell down,
From the sky,
She had blonde hair,
And a twinkle in her eye,

Her dress had a silver lining,
Her shoes were a pearly white,
She was truly shining,
She was the prettiest sight,

She told me stories,
From far, far away,
And about the planet,
We live on today,

After a while,
She had to go,
It was sad,
But I still know,

She's the bright star,
Up in space,
And she's always there,
To put a smile on your face.

Sarah James-Short (11)
The Globe Primary School, Lancing

Pizza

I love pizza,
Pizza is round,
It's not square.
I love pizza,
Some like lots of toppings,
I like it bare.
Thin crust,
Thick crust,
I really don't mind.
The best cheese is mozzarella,
I think you'll find,
I love pizza.

Henry Marchant (8)
The Globe Primary School, Lancing

My Smart Sister

My smart sister
Is great when doing homework.

She could be a teacher
For she is so great.

My smart sister,
Is great at everything.

She could be a doctor
For she is so great.

My smart sister
Is a great sister.

She could be the president
For she is so great.

I'm a lucky sister
For my sister is so great.

Olivia Cheung (9)
The Globe Primary School, Lancing

Scary Night

Scary, as scary, as scary can be.
If you dare walk into the scary forest,
You'll get a fright!
The spooky forest is black tonight,
There will be wolves, witches,
With slugs and snails
And the creepiest of snakes and spiders.
Scary, as scary, as scary can be.
Lightning flashes everywhere,
Where dragons and dinosaurs roam the land!
And all other things, too.
So remember you li'l kiddies,
Or you will face a painful doom!

Rooooaaaaarrrrrr!

Jay Southon (7) & Lewis James-Short (8)
The Globe Primary School, Lancing

The Little Brown Mouse

Have you ever heard my story
Of the little brown mouse?
He thought it would be smart
To live in Keira's dolls' house

So while the dolls were sleeping
He made himself a nest

The dolls were pleased to meet him
When they woke and found their guest

They hoped he would be happy
And freely run about
But when Keira saw him
She screamed and threw him out.

Ethan Taylor (8)
The Globe Primary School, Lancing

The Trojan Horse

We've won, we've won!
The Greeks have gone!
Oh no, oh no,
A wooden horse,
It's coming right for us!
Nooooooo!
There are people coming out of it!
Oh no, oh no!
Fire!
The city is gone!
I know we'll have to fight!
We haven't won!

Phoenix Grice & Saren Driscoll (9)
The Globe Primary School, Lancing

The Snowdrop

Shimmering in the moonlight,
Like a diamond in a case,
I look left, I look right and
There it is just staring at me.

Shimmering in the moonlight,
Like a star in the sky,
I look up, I look down and all around,
And there it is just sitting in the ground.

Shimmering in the moonlight,
I'm not a nasty person because
If I was I would have a nasty fright.

Terri Ballard (9)
The Globe Primary School, Lancing

Snowdrops

Snowdrops, snowdrops
White and dainty
Snowdrops, snowdrops
Show that summer's ahead.

Their stems are dainty
The one that is connecting the bud and the stem
You can hardly see at all.

They are pretty
They are white
Snowdrops, snowdrops
Are the best.

Melissa Shaw (9)
The Globe Primary School, Lancing

My Magical Birthday List

For my birthday I would like a rocket that goes to Mars
Because I've always wanted to meet a planet!
For my birthday I would like a computer
That when you type something in it works!
For my birthday I would like to perform in a panto!
I would like my teddies to come alive.
I would like to live in a world made of chocolate.
I would like to ride a unicorn.
I would like to be a deer and feel what it's like to have four legs.

This is what I would like for my birthday!

Milly Rose Marshall (8)
The Globe Primary School, Lancing

The Cyclops Poem

The Cyclops was funny, he had a big tummy
The big fierce giant went for a dig,
And after that he saw a pig.

He found a boy, his name was Troy,
He wanted to collect some more joy.

Ulysses came and he had a *big* name,
He wanted to destroy the boy called Troy.

He found the boy, his name was Troy,
He already had his happy joy!

Caitlin Wattam (8) & Lauren Redding (9)
The Globe Primary School, Lancing

Flamingos

Flamingos are pink
Flamingos are tall

They sleep standing up

But that's not all!

They can stand on one leg for a very long time

That's the end of my poem and I got it to rhyme.

Lauren Blann (8)
The Globe Primary School, Lancing

The Cyclops

One-eyed monster
Got a pole in his eye,
Went to sleep and,
Had to *die!*

Moved the rock
On bellies of sheep
Sailed away.
A no-eyed monster
Had to *die!*

Tess Bell & Ethan Gravett (8)
The Globe Primary School, Lancing

Swimming

Swimming is *fun!*
Swimming is in the sun
Swimming is hot
But it can't be steaming hot!

Swimming is lucky
But swimming is not mucky
Swimming is lots of things
But swimming is not you
Or is it?

Holly Atkinson (8)
The Globe Primary School, Lancing

Football Poem

Football, football
I love football.
It is the best
I have ever tried!
You score lots of goals.
Football, football
Gerrard is the
Best, best, best,
Football, football!

Hannah Schaffa & Connor Purcell (9)
The Globe Primary School, Lancing

For My Birthday

For my birthday I would like to have a car
For my birthday I would like to be
Tom Riddle Voldemort, the Dark Lord
For my birthday I want to watch Harry Potter and
The Deathly Hallows Part 1 and 2
For my birthday I would like to be Homer Simpson
For my birthday I would like 1000052 pounds!
For my birthday I would like to have a proper wand and sword.
For my birthday I would like to speak snake language!

Jay Southon (7)
The Globe Primary School, Lancing

Lonely Penguin

Lonely penguin swimming in the sea,
Would you like to swim like me?
Playing in the white, thick snow,
Please, please, say it will glow.

Lonely penguin all black and white,
On a silver fish she would nibble and bite.
Lonely penguin, I love you,
Lonely penguin, I love you too.

Caitlin Wattam (8)
The Globe Primary School, Lancing

Hot Chocolate

Hot chocolate nice and creamy,
I like it hot and steamy.

Hot chocolate lusciously brown,
It doesn't make me frown.

Hot chocolate in a pretty mug,
Although it makes me feel quite snug.

Marshmallows or not I like it nice and hot.

Lucy Drake (8)
The Globe Primary School, Lancing

Bees

Bees fly so fast,
So you can't see them.
Bees have sharp stingers on their bottoms,
But they really hurt when they sting you.
Bees fly so fast,
So you can't see them.
Bees are black and yellow,
Because that's their natural colour.

Billie-Jo Chandler (9)
The Globe Primary School, Lancing

The Cyclops

Two arms, two legs
A round big fat . . . head.

One eye, one eye
A big vicious . . . eye.

Ulysses, Ulysses,
He comes and pokes the big giant in the eye.

Holly Atkinson & George Bartlett (8)
The Globe Primary School, Lancing

Snowdrops

Snowdrops, snowdrops, shimmering white
Snowdrops, snowdrops, crisp and bright
Snowdrops, snowdrops, in the light
Snowdrops, snowdrops, clear in the night
Snowdrops, snowdrops, white in sight
Snowdrops, snowdrops, shimmering white.

Imogen Bromley (9)
The Globe Primary School, Lancing

Ulysses

'We've won, we've won,'
The Greeks have gone
But this giant wooden horse has come.
'We've won, we've won!'
Oh no soldiers from the belly of the horse will destroy Troy.
'We've lost, we've lost, we've lost!'

Terri Ballard & Jamie Peacock (9)
The Globe Primary School, Lancing

Little Penguin

Little penguin lives in the Arctic sea
Little penguin loves to swim like me
So there's nowhere else he'd rather be
He swims very deep
To find fish he can eat
He likes to explore and see who he can meet.

Tyla Guile (9)
The Globe Primary School, Lancing

Elves Dig

In mountain caves elves dig and toil
Mining brilliant gems from the blackest soil
Emeralds, diamonds, rubies are found in the waterfall
Then placed together on willow fronds
Magic bonds make fairy chains.

Phoebe Jean Mayhew (9)
The Globe Primary School, Lancing

Bebee's Box

In my box I will put
A star from above
A sparkle from the sun
An ear from the fluffiest cat

In the box goes
The secret of love
The skin from a hamster
The touch of a cloud

I will put into the box
The scent of roses
The smell of freshly baked chocolate cake
The taste of a sour apple

In the box I will put
The books of Harry Potter
The DVDs from Harry Potter
The taste of sour strawberries

In the box I will put
My family's happiness
The laughter of my best friends
The happiest memories I have ever had

I will put in my box
A sprinkle of friendship
The best things I have ever seen
And the shiny silver moon

In my box I will put
The saddest memories
The worst day ever
A precious ring from a relative

My box contains lots of memories
The sad, happy, best, worst.
A brown box with purple and blue wavy lines on will contain a lot.
My box is encrusted with the brightest ever rubies,
With spots of shiny diamonds poking out all around!

Briony Thornton (10)
West St Leonards Primary School, St Leonards-on-Sea

Meggy-Lou's Box
(Inspired by 'Magic Box' by Kit Wright)

In my box I will put,
My secrets that no one knows in the far corners,
My memories from everything I've ever done,
And a never-ending magical bar of chocolate.

In my box I will put,
All of my family who I'll never forget,
The smell of salt and vinegary chips from the chip shop,
And the miaow from my black, white and ginger cat Lola-Rose.

In my box I will put,
The cutest and most magical teddy that comes to life at night,
The pitch-black night sky with twinkling, sparkling stars,
And the deepest, softest, flakiest snow that comes past your knees.

In my box I will put,
The tastiest strawberry covered in sugar,
The lovely smelling lavender from the eerie woods,
And a drop of the crystal-blue sea which is everlasting.

In my box I will put,
My best friends who stick by me through thick and thin,
The funniest episode of SpongeBob SquarePants ever!
And the scariest, most exciting episode of Primeval ever!

In my box I will put,
The most boring day of school,
The most hilarious day of school ever,
And the meanest, strictest supply teacher ever.

In my box I will put,
Every battered shoe I've ever worn,
Every warming hug I've ever given,
And every word I've ever said, shouted and screamed.

My box is covered with purple silk with golden feathers
And encrusted with the reddest rubies, the bluest sapphires, the greenest emeralds, and the shiniest diamonds!

Megan-Louise Masters (11)
West St Leonards Primary School, St Leonards-on-Sea

The Achievement Box
(Inspired by 'Magic Box' by Kit Wright)

I will put in my box,
The greatest memories of doing an exam,
The fear of not getting something right,
Working so hard to do the splits,
Then being able to do them.

I will put in my box,
Coming second in the singing competition,
Looking at certificates and medals I've won,
Being able to jump 8ft high,
Next thing getting into the Royal Ballet School.

I will put in my box,
Meeting the Swan Lake cast,
Flying in the middle of solo dance,
Everyone shouting, 'Well done!' and 'Good show!'
All my family and friends being really proud of me.

I will put in my box,
Being Miss Howard's star of the day,
Making a brilliant handshake with Molly,
Everyone making a brilliant effort on a play and then getting a great applause,
Our whole year group making artwork.

My box is fashioned from,
Flowers on the top with magic wands,
Balloons and flowers on the side,
And the hinges are ballet ribbons.

I shall dance and sing in my box,
Let friends come and see shows in it,
I will sleep and eat in my box,
Look back at memories in my box..

Ellie Johnson (9)
West St Leonards Primary School, St Leonards-on-Sea

The Magic Box
(Inspired by 'Magic Box' by Kit Wright)

I will put in my box . . .
Four yellow beaches,
An animal from long, long ago,
One giant picture of people I have not yet met.

I will put in my box . . .
Six enormous horses,
A memory of last summer,
A horse on an enchanted island.

I will put in my box . . .
All eight planets in the solar system,
One memory of a friend in the past,
Seven dragons breathing fire.

I will put in my box . . .
Seven snowmen from last Christmas,
Two smiles from newborn babies,
Five snakes with harmless bites.

I will put in my box . . .
A picture of a stone wall,
A brave knight that rides a horse,
A newborn calf.

I will put in my box . . .
Four different seasons,
An electric eel swimming through the sea,
A very rare butterfly.

My box is fashioned from winter's night to summer's evening.

Beulah Griffiths Thompson (9)
West St Leonards Primary School, St Leonards-on-Sea

If I Had Wings!
(Inspired by 'If I Had Wings' by Pie Corbett)

If I had wings
I would dance on the clouds
And soar past the sun.

If I had wings
I would dive down to
Sydney Opera House and listen
To the sweet voices of the singers.

If I had wings
I would dive down to a eucalyptus tree
And have tea and a chat with a koala.

If I had wings
I would swoop up in the air
And bite a chunk of cloud that
Tastes like candyfloss.

If I had wings
I would go to Mars
And back in two seconds
And complete a world record.

If I had wings
I would explore the world
And seas and do anything
I wanted!
And no one
Could stop me!

Zoe Crowley (10)
West St Leonards Primary School, St Leonards-on-Sea

Chloe's Magic Box!
(Inspired by 'Magic Box' by Kit Wright)

I will put in my box
A snowman that talks and loves me
A chocolate bar the size of the London Eye
A big mansion for me and my family.

I will put in my box
The cutest dog, Bracken of course
I will bring my teddy dog that will come alive
The tinkle of a magic star.

I will put in my box
A shooting star at night
A bag of sweets as big as Australia
A horse that only talks and rides for me.

I will put in my box
A country that will listen to me
The smoothest stone on the beach
I will own Australia.

My box is half ice and half gold
With a twinkle of a star on the top and the sides of my box
The bottom will be filled with all my secrets.

Finally I will put in my box
My dog that will sing
Bruno Mars will give me a million pounds
Finally my loving family.

Chloe Fletcher (10)
West St Leonards Primary School, St Leonards-on-Sea

If I Had Wings
(Inspired by 'If I Had Wings' by Pie Corbett)

If I had wings
I would perch on stars
Watching people as small as ants.

If I had wings
I would cut through clouds
To find their hearts.

If I had wings
I would dance with the wind
Landing loop-the-loops.

If I had wings
I would discover a planet
To share with the world.

If I had wings
I would taste the fresh air
Running past my ears.

If I had wings
I would smell the moon
The most amazing smell in space.

If I had wings
I would touch the coral of the Great Barrier Reef
And save all the fish in the sea.

Imi Bennett (10)
West St Leonards Primary School, St Leonards-on-Sea

Sunset Secrets

It's never too hot and it's never too cold,
It's never too late and it's never too early.
I search and search for the secrets in my mind,
But I never find my
Sunset.

I run across the rainbow,
I skip along the sun.
I wait and wait,
But I never find my
Sunset.

I run and search,
Till I'm all worn out.
I need to catch my breath,
And I never find my sunset.

I find all bright colours,
From light shades to dark.
From high and low places,
But I never find my sunset.

Away in the distance,
I see far away.
My dreams and desires,
My sunset . . . here to stay!

Kira Jade Madge (11)
West St Leonards Primary School, St Leonards-on-Sea

The Australian Box
(Inspired by 'Magic Box' by Kit Wright)

I'll put in the box . . .
The fiery sun that burns the life out of you
And the huntsman spider that gives head massages.
I'll put in the box . . .
The climbing koala that gets your laundry off the line for you,
And a touch of koala's fur.
I'll put in the box . . .
The sand that tickles between your toes
And a jellyfish that refuses to wobble.

Rebecca Perkins (11)
West St Leonards Primary School, St Leonards-on-Sea

If I Had Wings
(Inspired by 'If I Had Wings' by Pie Corbett)

If I had wings
I'd escape the jaws of school
And give freedom to the world

If I had wings
I'd crack the moon in half
And take a half to a friend

If I had wings
I would taste the most
Fluffiest cloud on top of the world

If I had wings
I would dive down
The highest volcano

If I had wings
I'd catch the
Biggest fish in the sea

If I had wings
I would swim the
Seven seas

That's what I would do if I had wings.
What would you do if you had wings?

Rian McDonald (10)
West St Leonards Primary School, St Leonards-on-Sea

The Magic Box
(Inspired by 'Magic Box' by Kit Wright)

I will put in the box
The ho ho ho of Santa
The giggle of a spider
A gurgle of a fish

I will put in the box
The colours of a rainbow
The golden sand
And the sparkling blue sea

I will put in the box
My mountaineering hamster
My favourite teddy
And my first tooth

I will put in the box
My three weeks in China
A cat that roars
A fiery-eyed dragon that purrs

I will put in the box
My dog Cindy
My dog Freddie
And my heart.

Nadia Avery (10)
West St Leonards Primary School, St Leonards-on-Sea

If I Had Wings
(Inspired by 'If I Had Wings' by Pie Corbett)

If I had wings
I would glide
With the birds

If I had wings
I would stroll across the clouds
And bounce on them, like a trampoline

If I had wings
High in the skies
I would follow an aeroplane

If I had wings
I would shoot up to the moon
And claim my visit with a flag

If I had wings
I would shoot down
And grab a piece of coral from the Barrier Reef

If I had wings
I would hover over the towns and cities
Across the sea and land
And I'd wave to millions of people as I glided high.

Michael Amos (10)
West St Leonards Primary School, St Leonards-on-Sea

Olivia's Magic Box
(Inspired by 'Magic Box' by Kit Wright)

I will put in my box
A smell of cheese and pepperoni pizza,
A friendship island with lots of friends,
A smell of a book.

I will put in my box
A big fire,
The smell of smoke
A rainbow.

I will put in my box
A big elephant,
A best friend,
Miss Howard,
Mrs Dowling.

I will put in my box
Two red balloons,
The bright sun,
The smell of cheese.

My box is fashioned from flowers and stars.
I will eat an apple and sweets in my box.

Olivia Metalle (9)
West St Leonards Primary School, St Leonards-on-Sea

Magic Box
(Inspired by 'Magic Box' by Kit Wright)

I will put in my box
Magic wishes big and small,
A big unicorn with a sheet of stars under her feet,
The smell of big, pink, strawberry clouds.

I will put in my box,
A great wood which I can go to,
Animals that can talk to me,
A memory for when I grow old.

I will put in my box,
A big pink strawberry, many flavours,
A sample of the bluest skies,
A big picture of my friends and family.

I will put in my box,
Witches and wizards who cast spells,
Big stars shimmering so brightly,
A jar of fresh honey
A wild horse galloping on a warm summer night.

My box is fashioned from the most lovely thing you can imagine.
It is nice and you can store lots of things from your head.

Hannah Chapman (8)
West St Leonards Primary School, St Leonards-on-Sea

If I Had Wings
(Inspired by 'If I Had Wings' by Pie Corbett)

If I had wings
I would glide to the top of the clouds
And gaze all around England.

If I had wings
I would zoom like a bird
To the moon and sleep all night long.

If I had wings
I would explore all around the deepest sea and
Find the most popular fish.

If I had wings
I would shoot up above the Earth and float like
A rubber ring.

If I had wings
I would cut through the clouds and balance on them.

If I had wings
I would drop down through the Earth and find the
World's most beautiful plant.

I will open my box on a sunny day to remember my memories.

Bronwyn Kent (11)
West St Leonards Primary School, St Leonards-on-Sea

My Magic Box
(Inspired by 'Magic Box' by Kit Wright)

I will put in my box,
All of my happy days!
I would like super JLS to have just made up 'Everybody In Love'!
I would love to stroke my grandma's dog again but
Sadly he died!

I will put in my box
My very first fun birthday.
My loveable puppy's first day home when she was very small!
The taste of my creamy hot chocolate!

I will put in my box
The first time I ever went to Brownies!
The first time I was a bridesmaid!
My first snowy Christmas.

My box is fashioned from
Ice that comes from magical places
With snowflakes on the lid
And secrets in the corner.
I shall fly in my box
To Antarctica and ride on the polar bears.

Megan Green (8)
West St Leonards Primary School, St Leonards-on-Sea

India

India India
Exciting India,
India, India
Hot and spicy,
India, India
As big as a
Mountain,
India, India
One class
In a school
India, India
Fantastic
India.

Ryan Lucas (7)
West St Leonards Primary School, St Leonards-on-Sea

If I Had Wings
(Inspired by 'If I Had Wings' by Pie Corbett)

If I had wings
I would touch the eyebrows of Ayers Rock
And hover on air.

If I had wings
I would dive down into Earth
And explore the underground.

If I had wings
I would soar over the outback
And browse at the kangaroos.

If I had wings
I would zoom into the Great Barrier Reef
And steal all the fishes.

If I had wings
I would taste Earth's core
As hot as boiled water.

If I had wings
I would dream of strolling across the outback
And glide across the seas.

Layla Constable (10)
West St Leonards Primary School, St Leonards-on-Sea

My Magic Box
(Inspired by 'Magic Box' by Kit Wright)

I will put in the box
The largest garlic bread pizza,
Which sticks to my nose when I take the biggest bit I can do!
A cowboy on a broomstick,
And a witch on a white horse.

I will put in the box
A cream egg from Lee.
My large, loving bird called Sally, who I share my feelings with.

My box is fashioned from stars and the moon,
With monkeys on the lid and fluff in the corners.
I shall fly in my box through the white, fluffy clouds to Disneyland!

Jessica Avery (8)
West St Leonards Primary School, St Leonards-on-Sea

If I Had Wings
(Inspired by 'If I Had Wings' by Pie Corbett)

If I had wings
I would surf the sky
And eat the clouds as if they were candyfloss

If I had wings
I would dive into the Earth
And cannonball into Paris

If I had wings
I would swoop down into Australia
And touch the tongue of Sydney Opera House

If I had wings
I would shoot like a rocket into space
And grab the brightest star I could see

If I had wings
I would float through space
And observe the wonderful views

If I had wings
I would gaze back down to Earth And pretend nothing happened.

Sinead Bedwell (11)
West St Leonards Primary School, St Leonards-on-Sea

A Winter's Dream

The crackling fire at the roof of my mind,
The nightmare I glued to the back of my head.
The dreams that weaved through thick and thin,
On the cold winter's night.

The snow that falls on my secrets and dreams,
My sweet dreams made of ponies and trophies,
Crushed to the floor by schoolgirl fantasies,
On the cold winter's night.

The sun I long for on this gloomy night,
When I cuddle my pillow and sleep warm and tight,
The sound of my alarm ringing in my ears,
On the cold winter's night.

Megan Barnett (11)
West St Leonards Primary School, St Leonards-on-Sea

My Magic Box
(Inspired by 'Magic Box' by Kit Wright)

I will put into my box
The call of a lost dolphin,
The scent of a wet rose,
The last eclipse of a winter's day.

I will put into my box
A crystal ball containing forever-lasting light,
A wizard with a long silver beard,
An angel's glowing wing.

I will put into my box
One gem from the oldest crown,
Two squirts of the most expensive perfume,
Three stars from the midnight sky.

I will put into my box
My signed hardback book,
My first true love,
My findings on PGL.

My box is made of gold and feathers,
Encrusted with deep blue sapphires.

Jazmine Murray (11)
West St Leonards Primary School, St Leonards-on-Sea

The Mythical Box
(Inspired by 'Magic Box' by Kit Wright)

In my box I will put
A sprinkle of fairy dust from a secret fairy.

In my box you will seek
Wishes from a wishing tree.

In my box I will put
A colourful rainbow which fits round your foot.

In my box you will find
Stars from space from miles and miles.

My box is made of flowers and pixie dust
And the lid has a moon that tastes of chocolate.

Natalie Stoodley (11)
West St Leonards Primary School, St Leonards-on-Sea

India

India
India
Fabulous
India
Your sun is like a ball of fire
Your trees are wavy like grass.
Your food is sweet, fantastic and gorgeous.
Chewy, delicious, scrumptious.
Chilly, spectacular food.
Yummy giant bread.
Your weather is boiling,
Hot and warm
With rainy raindrops
The schools are
Like birds flying in the sky.
Animals are big as trees.
The rivers
Are blowing
In the
Wind.

Layla Fisher (8)
West St Leonards Primary School, St Leonards-on-Sea

The Roman Box
(Inspired by 'Magic Box' by Kit Wright)

I will put in my Roman box . . .

The shouting of a centurion,
The roar of a lion crawling at a gladiator,
Romans stomping and charging.

I will put in my Roman box . . .

The clanging of swords and shields,
Shrieking and screams from a scared crowd,
The roar from an angry army.

I will put in my Roman box . . .

The steam from the Roman baths,
And the silky touch of the water.

Sophie O'Hara (8)
West St Leonards Primary School, St Leonards-on-Sea

My Random Box
(Inspired by 'Magic Box' by Kit Wright)

I will put in my box,
The sound of a racing car tyre screeching down a steep hill,
The view of the bright sun beaming down on a tropical island,
The aroma of a pancake flipping through the humid air.

I will put in my box,
The roar of a brand new sports car's engine zooming,
The happiness of Chelsea's victory of the FA Cup
The taste of oozing cheese pizza touching my tongue.

I will put in my box,
The strong vibrations of a mobile phone in my pocket,
The pain of a football smacking me in the face,
The sight of a plane crashing head-first into the ground.

I will sail in my box in a wooden, creaky pirate ship,
Under the glowing moon in starry night's sky.

My box is fashioned from plastic hinges and gleaming gold but,
Secretly, it has solid layers of sharp steel, so beware!

Hamza Husain (8)
West St Leonards Primary School, St Leonards-on-Sea

My Magic Box!
(Inspired by 'Magic Box' by Kit Wright)

I will put in the box . . .
The first season of the year
The Christmas spirit
And the autumn mist.

I will put in the box . . .
The sound of EastEnders drama
My best teacher Mrs Chapman
And a kiss from my mum.

I will put in the box . . .
The brain of a clever parrot
The legs of a ferocious mountain lion
And wings of a Chinese dragon.

My magic box is the best box ever.

Kiera Dixon (10)
West St Leonards Primary School, St Leonards-on-Sea

Dionne's Magic Box
(Inspired by 'Magic Box' by Kit Wright)

I will put in my box
Trees that could talk and walk around
A big hug for my brother
And a kiss for my mum

I will put in my box
The smell of new cut grass
The smell of bubbly bath
And the smell of a roast dinner on a Sunday

I will put in my box
The taste of hot chocolate dripping down my throat
The taste of chocolate melting on the tip of my tongue
And the taste of water from Tesco Express

I will put in my box
The sight of my best friend smiling whilst waving goodbye
The sight of my baby's first smile
The sight of my trees blowing in the autumn breeze.

Dionne Clarke (10)
West St Leonards Primary School, St Leonards-on-Sea

India

India
India
Sweet and sour.
Messy, messy
Homes are messy
Spicy, spicy
Food is spicy
Sparkly, sparkly
Clothes are
Sparkly.
Boiling,
Boiling,
The sun
Is boiling
India
India.

Hermione White (8)
West St Leonards Primary School, St Leonards-on-Sea

If I Had Wings I Would . . .
(Inspired by 'If I Had Wings' by Pie Corbett)

If I had wings,
I would see far, far away,
I would smell piles of haystacks
Scattered across a farm.
I would smell gas from a cosy hot air balloon ride.

If I had wings,
I would see stunning views,
And waterfalls dripping off a mountain.
I would see rippling grassland
As wide as a dazzling ocean.

If I had wings,
I would fly over mountains and lakes too.
I would see the lights, from the city,
Light up as bright as the sun rising.
I would take a glide along the beach
And feel a gentle breeze in my feathers.

Lydia Smith (10)
West St Leonards Primary School, St Leonards-on-Sea

If I Had Wings
(Inspired by 'If I Had Wings' by Pie Corbett)

If I had wings,
I would fly high and breathe the crystal-like air
While staring at the stunning views.

If I had wings,
I would stare at the hot air balloons just drifting
With the wind
Smelling the lovely, sparkling waterfall down below.

If I had wings,
I would gaze at the small antlike people and say
Hello from high above
And they would wave their reply whilst I was
Drifting through the air.

Joy Overbury (11)
West St Leonards Primary School, St Leonards-on-Sea

My Magic Box
(Inspired by 'Magic Box' by Kit Wright)

I will put in my box
The amazing memories when I was small,
The noise of my bunny jumping in the cage,
The photos in the gold foil waiting for me to open!

I will put in my box
The wonderful love from my family,
The ocean that roars at night,
The delightful JLS singers that sing 'Beat Again!'

I will put in my box
The money that my mum puts in my money box,
The sound of my dogs barking,
The hugs from my loving grandad!

My box is fashioned from gold and silver with red hearts on the lid,
Sweets in the corners!

I shall fly in my box over the castles and the soft clouds and into space!

Bethany McDonald (8)
West St Leonards Primary School, St Leonards-on-Sea

The Australian Box
(Inspired by 'Magic Box' by Kit Wright)

I will put in my box . . .

The ash from the scary bush fires,
The lovely and horrid notes from the didgeridoo,
A touch of a scared newborn koala.

I will put in my box . . .

The wind from a crazy spinning boomerang,
The first sight of the world-famous Sydney Opera House,
A part of the fiery sun that tastes like a hot pepper sauce.

My box has gold and silver stars
With a dark background that I will swim with ocean to ocean.
Then I will crawl through warm golden sand on an island called Australia!

Emily Louise Hendy (10)
West St Leonards Primary School, St Leonards-on-Sea

The Australian Box
(Inspired by 'Magic Box' by Kit Wright)

I will put in the box,
The sound of tapping feet of Australian dancers,
The smell of Australian food from a distance,
And risen sun upon my face,

I will put in the box,
The lights shining in my eyes from the Sydney Opera House,
The grand height of the Sydney Harbour Bridge,
And the amazing ruby colour of Ayers Rock,

I will put in the box,
The touch of a koala's fur,
The sound of angry wombats,
And the fiery colour of the kangaroos,

My box is filled with Aboriginal art on the top
And boomerangs hanging out of the corners.
My box is the feeling of Australia!

Megan Croucher (11)
West St Leonards Primary School, St Leonards-on-Sea

Rotten Romans
(Inspired by 'Magic Box' by Kit Wright)

I will put in the box . . .
Five drips of blood from a sharp sword!
Also all the love from Cupid.
And roar of a lion chasing a brave gladiator.

I will put in the box . . .
The sharpest deadly Gladius chopping someone's head off!
Also, the last word of an unbeatable gladiator.
And the outrageous gigantic shield.

I will put in the box . . .
The scream of someone dying!
Also, the deadly Gladius!
A gladiator screaming going through a trapdoor!

My box is fashioned by blood and memories on the lid
And deathtraps in the corners!
I will fight in my box in 1966.

Joanne Perkins (9)
West St Leonards Primary School, St Leonards-on-Sea

Maddie's Workshop

Featured Author:

Maddie Stewart

Maddie is a children's writer, poet and author who currently lives in Coney Island, Northern Ireland.

Maddie has 5 published children's books, 'Cinders', 'Hal's Sleepover', 'Bertie Rooster', 'Peg' and 'Clever Daddy'. Maddie uses her own unpublished work to provide entertaining, interactive poems and rhyming stories for use in her workshops with children when she visits schools, libraries, arts centres and book festivals.

Favourites are 'Silly Billy, Auntie Millie' and 'I'm a Cool, Cool Kid'. Maddie works throughout Ireland from her home in County Down. She is also happy to work from a variety of bases in England. She has friends and family, with whom she regularly stays, in Leicester, Bedford, London and Ashford (Kent). Maddie's workshops are aimed at 5-11-year-olds. Check out Maddie's website for all her latest news and free poetry resources **www.maddiestewart.com**.

Read on to pick up some fab writing tips!

Nonsense Workshop

If you find silliness fun, you will love nonsense poems. Nonsense poems might describe silly things, or people, or situations, or, any combination of the three.

For example:

When I got out of bed today,
both my arms had run away.
I sent my feet to fetch them back.
When they came back, toe in hand
I realised what they had planned.
They'd made the breakfast I love most,
buttered spider's eggs on toast.

**One way to find out if you enjoy nonsense poems
is to start with familiar nursery rhymes.
Ask your teacher to read them out,
putting in the names of some children in your class.**

Like this: Troy and Jill went up the hill
to fetch a pail of water.
Troy fell down
and broke his crown
and Jill came tumbling after.

If anyone is upset at the idea of using their name, then don't use it.

Did you find this fun?

Maddie's Workshop

**Now try changing a nursery rhyme.
Keep the rhythm and the rhyme style, but invent a silly situation.**

Like this: Hickory Dickory Dare
a pig flew up in the air.
The clouds above
gave him a shove
Hickory Dickory Dare.

Or this: Little Miss Mabel
sat at her table
eating a strawberry pie
but a big, hairy beast
stole her strawberry feast
and made poor little Mabel cry.

How does your rhyme sound if you put your own name in it?

Another idea for nonsense poems is to pretend letters are people and have them do silly things.

For example:

Mrs A	Mrs B	Mrs C
Lost her way	Dropped a pea	Ate a tree

**To make your own 'Silly People Poem', think of a word to use.
To show you an example, I will choose the word 'silly'.
Write your word vertically down the left hand side of your page.
Then write down some words which rhyme
with the sound of each letter.**

S mess, dress, Bess, chess, cress
I eye, bye, sky, guy, pie, sky
L sell, bell, shell, tell, swell, well
L " " " " " " (" means the same as written above)
Y (the same words as those rhyming with I)

Use your rhyming word lists to help you make up your poem.

Mrs S made a mess
Mrs I ate a pie
Mrs L rang a bell
Mrs L broke a shell
Mrs Y said 'Bye-bye.'

You might even make a 'Silly Alphabet' by using all the letters of the alphabet.

It is hard to find rhyming words for all the letters. H, X and W are letters which are hard to match with rhyming words. I'll give you some I've thought of:

H - cage, stage, wage (close but not perfect)
X - flex, specs, complex, Middlesex
W - trouble you, chicken coop, bubble zoo

However, with nonsense poems, you can use nonsense words. You can make up your own words.

To start making up nonsense words you could try mixing dictionary words together. Let's make up some nonsense animals.

Make two lists of animals. (You can include birds and fish as well.)

Your lists can be as long as you like. These are lists I made:

elephant   kangaroo
tiger   penguin
lizard   octopus
monkey   chicken

Now use the start of an animal on one list and substitute it for the start of an animal from your other list.

I might use the start of oct/opus ... oct and substitute it for the end of l/izard to give me a new nonsense animal ... an octizard.
I might swap the start of monk/ey ... monk with the end of kang/aroo
To give me another new nonsense animal ... a monkaroo.

What might a monkaroo look like? What might it eat?

You could try mixing some food words in the same way, to make up nonsense foods.

cabbage   potatoes
lettuce   parsley
bacon   crisps

Cribbage, bacley, and lettatoes are some nonsense foods made up from my lists.

Let's see if I can make a nonsense poem about my monkaroo.

Maddie's Workshop

My monkaroo loves bacley.
He'll eat lettatoes too
But his favourite food is cribbage
Especially if it's blue.

Would you like to try and make up your own nonsense poem?

Nonsense words don't have to be a combination of dictionary words. They can be completely 'made up'. You can use nonsense words to write nonsense sonnets, or list poems or any type of poem you like.

Here is a poem full of nonsense words:

I melly micked a turdle
and flecked a pendril's tum.
I plotineyed a shugat
and dracked a pipin's plum.

Ask your teacher to read it putting in some children's names instead of the first I, and he or she instead of the second I.

Did that sound funny?

You might think that nonsense poems are just silly and not for the serious poet. However poets tend to love language. Making up your own words is a natural part of enjoying words and sounds and how they fit together. Many poets love the freedom nonsense poems give them. Lots and lots of very famous poets have written nonsense poems. I'll name some: **Edward Lear**, **Roger McGough**, **Lewis Carroll**, **Jack Prelutsky** and **Nick Toczek**. Can you or your teacher think of any more? For help with a class nonsense poem or to find more nonsense nursery rhymes look on my website, **www.maddiestewart.com**. Have fun! Maddie Stewart.

Poetry Techniques

Here is a selection of poetry techniques with examples

Metaphors & Similes

A *metaphor* is when you describe your subject *as* something else, for example: 'Winter is a cruel master leaving the servants in a bleak wilderness' whereas a *simile* describes your subject *like* something else i.e. 'His blue eyes are like ice-cold puddles' or 'The flames flickered like eyelashes'.

Personification

This is to simply give a personality to something that is not human, for example 'Fear spreads her uneasiness around' or 'Summer casts down her warm sunrays'.

Imagery

To use words to create mental pictures of what you are trying to convey, your poem should awaken the senses and make the reader feel like they are in that poetic scene ...
'The sky was streaked with pink and red as shadows cast across the once-golden sand'.
'The sea gently lapped the shore as the palm trees rustled softly in the evening breeze'.

Assonance & Alliteration

Alliteration uses a repeated constant sound and this effect can be quite striking: 'Smash, slippery snake slithered sideways'.
Assonance repeats a significant vowel or vowel sound to create an impact: 'The pool looked cool'.

Poetry Techniques

Repetition

By repeating a significant word the echo effect can be a very powerful way of enhancing an emotion or point your poem is putting across.
'The blows rained down, down,
Never ceasing,
Never caring
About the pain,
The pain'.

Onomatopoeia

This simply means you use words that sound like the noise you are describing, for example 'The rain *pattered* on the window' or 'The tin can *clattered* up the alley'.

Rhythm & Metre

The *rhythm* of a poem means 'the beat', the sense of movement you create. The placing of punctuation and the use of syllables affect the *rhythm* of the poem. If your intention is to have your poem read slowly, use double, triple or larger syllables and punctuate more often, where as if you want to have a fast-paced read use single syllables, less punctuation and shorter sentences.
If you have a regular rhythm throughout your poem this is known as *metre*.

Enjambment

This means you don't use punctuation at the end of your line, you simply let the line flow on to the next one. It is commonly used and is a good word to drop into your homework!

Tone & Lyric

The poet's intention is expressed through their *tone*. You may feel happiness, anger, confusion, loathing or admiration for your poetic subject. Are you criticising or praising? How you feel about your topic will affect your choice of words and therefore your *tone*. For example 'I *loved* her', 'I *cared* for her', 'I *liked* her'.
If you write the poem from a personal view or experience this is referred to as a *lyrical* poem. A good example of a lyrical poem is Seamus Heaney's 'Mid-term Break' or any sonnet!

All About Shakespeare

Try this fun quiz with your family, friends or even in class!

1. Where was Shakespeare born?

....

2. Mercutio is a character in which Shakepeare play?

....

3. Which monarch was said to be 'quite a fan' of his work?

....

4. How old was he when he married?

....

5. What is the name of the last and 'only original' play he wrote?

....

6. What are the names of King Lear's three daughters?

....

7. Who is Anne Hathaway?

....

All About Shakespeare

8. Which city is the play 'Othello' set in?

....

9. Can you name 2 of Shakespeare's 17 comedies?

....

10. 'This day is call'd the feast of Crispian: He that outlives this day, and comes safe home, Will stand a tip-toe when this day is nam'd, and rouse him at the name of Crispian' is a quote from which play?

....

11. Leonardo DiCaprio played Romeo in the modern day film version of Romeo and Juliet. Who played Juliet in the movie?

....

12. Three witches famously appear in which play?

....

13. Which famous Shakespearean character is Eric in the image to the left?

....

14. What was Shakespeare's favourite poetic form?

....

Answers are printed on the last page of the book, good luck!

If you would rather try the quiz online,
you can do so at www.youngwriters.co.uk.

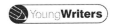

Poetry Activity

Word Soup

To help you write a poem, or even a story, on any theme, you should create word soup!

If you have a theme or subject for your poem, base your word soup on it.
If not, don't worry, the word soup will help you find a theme.

To start your word soup you need ingredients:

- Nouns (names of people, places, objects, feelings, i.e. Mum, Paris, house, anger)
- Colours
- Verbs ('doing words', i.e. kicking, laughing, running, falling, smiling)
- Adjectives (words that describe nouns, i.e. tall, hairy, hollow, smelly, angelic)

We suggest at least 5 of each from the above list, this will make sure your word soup has plenty of choice. Now, if you have already been given a theme or title for your poem, base your ingredients on this. If you have no idea what to write about, write down whatever you like, or ask a teacher or family member to give you a theme to write about.

Poetry Activity

Making Word Soup

Next, you'll need a sheet of paper.
Cut it into at least 20 pieces. Make sure the pieces are big enough to write your ingredients on, one ingredient on each piece of paper.
Write your ingredients on the pieces of paper.
Shuffle the pieces of paper and put them all in a box or bowl
- something you can pick the paper out of without looking at the words.
Pick out 5 words to start and use them to write your poem!

Example:

Our theme is winter. Our ingredients are:
- Nouns: snowflake, Santa, hat, Christmas, snowman.
- Colours: blue, white, green, orange, red.
- Verbs: ice-skating, playing, laughing, smiling, wrapping.
- Adjectives: cold, tall, fast, crunchy, sparkly.

**Our word soup gave us these 5 words:
snowman, red, cold, hat, fast and our poem goes like this:**

It's a *cold* winter's day,
My nose and cheeks are *red*
As I'm outside, building my *snowman*,
I add a *hat* and a carrot nose to finish,
I hope he doesn't melt too *fast*!

**Tip: add more ingredients to your word soup
and see how many different poems you can write!**

**Tip: if you're finding it hard to write a poem with
the words you've picked, swap a word with another one!**

**Tip: try adding poem styles and techniques,
such as assonance or haiku to your soup for an added challenge!**

Writers Information

We hope you have enjoyed reading this book - and that you will continue to enjoy it in the coming years.

If you like reading and writing poetry drop us a line, or give us a call, and we'll send you a free information pack.

Alternatively, if you would like to order further copies of this book or any of our other titles, then please give us a call or log onto our website at www.youngwriters.co.uk.

Young Writers Information
Remus House
Coltsfoot Drive
Peterborough
PE2 9BF
Tel: (01733) 890066
Fax: (01733) 313524

Email: info@youngwriters.co.uk

Shakespeare Quiz Answers

1. Stratford-upon-Avon **2.** Romeo and Juliet **3.** James I **4.** 18 **5.** The Tempest **6.** Regan, Cordelia and Goneril **7.** His wife **8.** Venice **9.** All's Well That Ends Well, As You Like It, The Comedy of Errors, Cymbeline, Love's Labour's Lost, Measure for Measure, The Merchant of Venice, The Merry Wives of Windsor, A Midsummer Night's Dream, Much Ado About Nothing, Pericles - Prince of Tyre, The Taming of the Shrew, The Tempest, Twelfth Night, The Two Gentlemen of Verona, Troilus & Cressida, The Winter's Tale **10.** Henry V **11.** Claire Danes **12.** Macbeth **13.** Hamlet **14.** Sonnet